PISTOL PACKIN'
PREACHERS

PISTOL PACKIN' PREACHERS

BARBARA BARTON

A REPUBLIC OF TEXAS PRESS BOOK
TAYLOR TRADE PUBLISHING
Lanham • New York • Dallas • Boulder • Toronto • Oxford

A REPUBLIC OF TEXAS PRESS BOOK

Published by Taylor Trade Publishing
An imprint of The Rowman & Littlefield Publishing Group, Inc.
4501 Forbes Boulevard, Suite 200
Lanham, Maryland 20706

Distributed by NATIONAL BOOK NETWORK

Library of Congress Cataloging-in-Publication Data

Barton, Barbara, 1940–
  Pistol packin' preachers / Barbara Barton. — 1st Taylor Trade Pub. ed.
    p. cm.
  "A Republic of Texas Press book."
  Includes bibliographical references and index.
  ISBN 1-58979-200-9 (pbk. : alk. paper)
  1. Texas—Church history. 2. Texas—Biography. I. Title.
  BR555.T4B375 2005
  277.64'081—dc22

2004027823

Dedicated to my grandchildren:
Meagan, Justin and Cathy

CONTENTS

ILLUSTRATIONS

FOREWORD

As pioneers pushed the frontiers westward, Bible-toting circuit preachers either rode with them or followed close behind. Often they carried a pistol in their saddlebags along with the scriptures, for they might face Indians or outlaws in addition to the sometimes-hostile elements to carry the word of God to the farthest edges of civilization. Occasionally the pistol lay on the pulpit along with the Bible to guarantee that a resistant flock listened to the message.

Barbara Barton's book relates the life stories of many early-day ministers who frequently risked life and limb to answer their calling. They were a disparate group, often having little in common except their missionary zeal and a willingness to endure extreme hardship in the Lord's service. A few literally died in the saddle. Others simply wore themselves out, traveling hundreds of miles a month ministering to their far-flung congregations.

The earliest Protestant ministers who immigrated into Mexican Texas in the footsteps of Stephen F. Austin risked prison for preaching their brand of the word. Mexican law forbade any religion except Catholicism. Many a Methodist or Baptist preacher kept one eye out for Mexican troops while he gave his sermon. Ministers rode among the ranks of those soldiers who fought for Texas independence, and years later others would ride with Confederate units in the Civil War.

Often a preacher was called upon to administer medical assistance as well as spiritual guidance. Many studied the healing arts as practiced in that time and became proficient doctors.

It was not unusual in early days for a circuit rider to conduct services in private homes or in the open, beneath shade trees or under crude brush arbors. Now and then they commandeered the use of a saloon, which might be the only building in town large enough to accommodate the crowd. The first real church in a frontier town most often resulted from a minister's diligent work in raising funds and soliciting volunteer labor from those who would become the congregation, and even from sinners who never would. When someone objected to accepting money from gamblers and saloonkeepers, the response might be that it had worked for the devil long enough, and it was time to put it to work for the Lord.

All too often, once a church was constructed the minister received a call to move on and repeat the process in another town or towns in need of the word. He built the church, then was honor-bound to leave it. But in so doing, he left a legacy of faith and commitment.

Today, when so many have lost their moral compass and there seem no longer to be absolutes of right and wrong, we can learn much from these men of great faith who endured all manner of sacrifice to answer the Lord's call and spread His teachings to the multitudes.

Elmer Kelton, author of *The Time It Never Rained*

CIRCUIT RIDERS IN TEXAS

The Lone Star State was once known as the place "where the Godly could battle 'the devil' on his own ground." Preachers confronted dangerous outlaws and Indians as well as wild animals and Texas's unpredictable weather. Most of these servants of God, dressed in pastoral black, preached from the Holy Book under tabernacles and in homes while traveling many dusty miles between the two. The remainder of the preacher's time was devoted to plowing his crops and tending his cattle in an effort to make ends meet. Preachers' salaries were nothing to write home about.

These Godly men, usually riding a bony horse with its ribs showing or pulling a cart by themselves, clearly affected men's lives with their message. They preached Leviticus 19:18, "Love your neighbor as yourself" as well as Acts 16:31, "Believe on the Lord Jesus and thou shalt be saved." More than a few parsons found themselves looking down an outlaw's gun barrel, but their messages changed many a wayward man's life.

The preacher's influence built schools, fought for the temperance movement and helped maintain law and order from the Red River to the Rio Grande. Brother L. R. Millican wore a deputy sheriff's badge. Brother Bill Robinson and Brother George Slaughter founded a school, the Brazos Institute, in 1859. David Ayres taught children in his home. Some preachers spoke out against slavery only to find their necks in the hangman's noose.

In the early years of Texas's development, parsons also filled in as schoolteachers and doctors. Many preachers found themselves also holding the title of chaplain at Texas's remote forts. They were among the few educated people moving among the citizens, so people responded to their leadership.

Similarly, Catholic padres, many from Europe, brought Christianity to the people living along the isolated Rio Grande region as well as other areas of Texas. They helped build schools and one priest, Father Pierre Keralum, was an excellent architect who designed churches.

The preacher, in his pastoral black, ministered to his flocks' body as well as their mind and spirit. Parsons accomplished all of this by sometimes raising their own gun against outlaws, Indians and other dangers so they could help tame this country called Texas.

ACKNOWLEDGMENTS

The publication of *Pistol Packin' Preachers* is possible only because of the number of people who have helped me in my quest to tell the story of our early-day preachers. Writers Ross McSwain and Elmer Kelton have encouraged me on my road to printing a book such as this. I appreciate Elmer taking the time to write a foreword to this book.

Many thanks to Suzanne Campbell, head of the Ralph P. Chase West Texas Collection at Angelo State University's Porter Henderson Memorial Library and her assistant Alex Cano; Becky Brackin, community news editor of the *San Angelo Standard Times*; Georgie Boyce, assistant photo archivist, of the Texas Wendish Heritage Museum Archives at Serbin, Texas; Fort Concho Museum at San Angelo, Texas; Margaret Schlankey of the Austin History Center in Austin, Texas; Linda Briscoe Myers, assistant curator of the Harry Ransom Humanities Research Center at the University of Texas, Austin, Texas; and T. J. Meyers and Martha Bell with the archives of the First Methodist Church of San Angelo, Texas.

A special thanks is given to my artist sister Sharon Gentry; Mary Jane Pettijohn of Comanche, Texas, granddaughter of Reverend William Robertson and her daughter Patsy Mears; Walter Clay Dixon, historical author of Fort Worth, Texas; the museum director at Paisano Baptist Encampment at Alpine, Texas; and my husband Lewis for many snapshots taken on our journeys chasing circuit riders.

I also want to thank Janet Harris, the Republic of Texas Press editor, who worked so patiently with me to make the book a reality.

1

BIBLES BROUGHT TO TEXAS:
1829–1835

Texas immigrants, whether scalawags running from the law or men with lily-white souls carrying Bibles, usually came into Texas by way of Louisiana or Arkansas. As their wagons rambled into Tejas country, immigrants saw a canopy of thick pine trees near creeks and lakes bubbling with fresh water. Deer and rabbits scampered through the undergrowth as wagons trudged along, so women passengers took note of the possibilities for the next meal. Meanwhile, the men sized up the plentiful trees they could use for lean-tos and later cabins. Some immigrants came alone, and others brought the wife, kids and rocking chair along with the feather bed, every belonging they could either throw into the wagon or tie onto the sides with rawhide.

Most immigrants desired a new start. Maybe life had not been too pleasant for them in Kentucky, Georgia or Ohio. By 1820 they had heard of a rough and ready Moses Austin who petitioned the Mexican government to let him bring 300 families to settle Tejas country. As he received permission to enter, the migration to this new land commenced, and many frontiersmen turned their horses in the southwesterly direction. Some men like Sumner Bacon started west without knowing where they would put down roots. This young man came westward with gun in hand like other immigrants. Many more firearms than Bibles crossed the boundary line of Tejas country in the early 1800s.

Rev. Sumner Bacon, as he was later called, not only packed a six-gun, he also eventually supplied the gunpowder, for the Texas War of Independence, that is. However, as a young man born in Auburn, Massachusetts, Bacon thought little about fighting any battles, especially those on Texas soil. His life was secure and serene, even rather genteel as he attended society functions in Auburn.

Then his father died in 1809, and Sumner Bacon's buggy flipped. Nothing was the same from that date. After the funeral, Bacon's family directed him toward the halls of higher education. Twenty-year-old Sumner was expected to be a college lad and graduate as a lawyer or doctor, but the wanderlust hit him pretty hard. Experiences awaiting over the next hill enticed him to leave home, so Bacon strapped on a gun and headed southwest for several years of meandering from place to place.

He must have thought a soldier's life looked interesting because at Fort Smith, Arkansas, Sumner joined the U.S. Army. As a soldier, Sumner Bacon drilled and took orders from his sergeant in 1823 and 1824. But when his service time expired, Bacon quickly switched a soldier's garb for buckskin pants and a hunting shirt. A family there in Arkansas hired the ex-soldier as a day laborer, and he seemed content to plow fields and chop wood for two years.

After a stay with them, Bacon again grew restless. Although young men like him looked for adventure as they traveled, Bacon found himself in a very different scenario one night. He went to an open-air revival and sat sedately on a pew at a Cumberland Presbyterian revival in Arkansas. Surprisingly, when the preacher pounded the pulpit and spoke of God's "power to throw you into hell," Bacon stepped onto the "sawdust road." He asked for forgiveness of his sins and became a Christian convert. At the outdoor revivals, people sprinkled sawdust on the ground to settle the dirt.

In his heart, Bacon felt that he wanted to preach the gospel, but men of the cloth were expected to become educated, and that ominous idea of being tied to the classroom gnawed at his insides again. Bacon had escaped college once in Massachusetts, and now the Cumberland Presbytery was preaching the idea of more education to new "wannabe" ministers like him. Church officials insisted that he clean up his grammar and spelling. They felt that two years of schooling would be sufficient to enable him to preach the Lord's message in a good sermon.

Bacon said, "No thank you" to school and began preaching his version of the gospel. He spoke with great enthusiasm, but his mouth invariably spat out profanity as often as it spoke psalms of comfort, probably due to his stay in the army. Several of the older Arkansas preachers criticized his delivery and suggested that Bacon was somewhat "erratic." Chastened, Rev. Sumner Bacon headed to Texas in 1829.

While this young man rode toward Tejas country, Moses Austin busily worked with the many immigrant families he brought into the Providence of Texas. He asked Don Antonio Martinez, governor of Texas, to let him bring families to live in this country as Tejas citizens. When Martinez agreed to this move, he stipulated that all colonists should be Roman Catholics or agree to become so before entering Spanish Territory. Such a decree put preachers like Sumner in deep trouble because he would not make his Presbyterian sermons imitate the Catholic Father's recitations.

Rev. William Smith was another preacher who protested against this decree. He said, "Men never become religious by contract or compulsion. Yet such was the law." Many of these families, following Austin to Texas, knew they were not Catholics and realized their marriages were considered null and void by the Spanish authorities.

Another problem with the Catholic ultimatum was the fact that when a young couple wanted to get married in Texas, they often had trouble locating the priest. The padres traveled large circuits in order to reach everybody, but they did not see some communities for many months or for as long as a year. Another drawback to a marriage in Texas was the $24 fee that the Catholic Church charged to marry a couple. This sum was more money than many young couples had. A type of Yankee ingenuity developed to work around the marriage problem.

By this makeshift system, young couples registered at the alcalde's office and had him draw up a bond to avail themselves of the priest's services when he visited their community on his next journey. Then the couple would consider themselves married. But this arrangement developed into some strange situations.

When the priest finally made his way to the couple's town to perform the wedding ceremony, toddlers might greet him and witness their mother's and dad's marriage ceremony. Conversely, divorces were also arranged through the same office. Since the time between the visit to the alcalde, or mayor, and the arrival of the priest was very long, some couples decided on an easy divorce when things did not work out between them. They simply went to the mayor's office, demanded their bond, tore it up and went their merry way—divorced.

Into this new land rode Sumner Bacon, small of stature but wanting to spread his brand of Protestant religion in a big way. His rough language blended well with the sharp words swapped between new Texas citizens, so he thought he could preach to these citizens with ease. He wrote Stephen Austin requesting to be a chaplain in his Texas colony, but Austin politely refused his intentions. At this time, Bacon's head hung low as he rode his horse toward East Texas. No one seemed to want an uneducated preacher like him although he had good intentions to save the world from sin.

In 1830 the Catholic Church also forbade anyone to distribute Bibles to Protestants in Texas. Bacon was soon to find out that priests and bishops were powerfully rough on anyone dispersing words from the Good Book since Catholicism dictated the proper way to teach the Bible in this region. To his consternation, Bacon found that the Mexican government controlled every man's worship. However, he defied the law. He began expounding the scriptures as an itinerant Presbyterian circuit rider the next year and slipped quietly into churches located around Shelby and Nacogdoches counties, areas in northeast Texas.

As Sumner Bacon traveled alone in East Texas, several rough characters attacked him, knocked him off his horse, and worked him over with their fists. It was obvious to the preacher that his adversaries wanted him dead. But now that he was a minister, he hesitated to pull his gun on them. Bacon asked the men instead if he could pray for them before they finished the job of killing him. After he called on the Almighty, the ruffians repented and became his good friends.

His new acquaintances were originally the most notorious horse thieves of the area. When the robbers came home, their cold-hearted mother asked why they did not kill the minister when they had the chance. The ruffians replied, "We never saw such a man. We would as soon kill our own father as him."

In this same region of East Texas, one day Rev. Bacon preached salvation's plan. His speech, showing deep concentration aimed at the souls of his outdoor audience, was interrupted when he saw some hell-raising cowboys riding toward his congregation. These men had the same idea as Bacon's earlier visitors: they decided the parson needed killing. Just as Bacon thought he was going to meet his Maker for sure this time, up rode his two new friends, the horse thieves, and stopped the lynching.

From 1829 until 1833, Bacon toured the Texas trails as an itinerant preacher, showing up at any meeting where people would listen to the gospel. Sometimes he held a two- or three-day meeting in a nearby tabernacle. Once he and Needham J. Alford planned a church revival near the present town of Milam in the spring of 1832. When they spread the word about the meeting, some people could hardly wait to attend while the prospect of such a gathering aggravated others.

James Gaines, the Sabine Ferry owner, did not want the preachers to stage their revival. He was influential in the neighborhood because his ferryboat was important to travelers as well as the people who lived nearby. He provided a good way to cross the Sabine River. This crossing, part of the Old San Antonio Road, had been in existence since 1795. James Gaines bought the ferry in 1819 from Michael Crow who had purchased it in 1796 when it was called the El Paso de Charlan. This means of crossing the river had been around for a long time.

James Gaines, watchful of any Texans staging an uprising whether it was political or religious, thought the revival was an overt act that defied the local rules and must be stopped at once. He gathered several men to help him take care of the preachers.

While Gaines and his men stood ready to oppose the "men of the cloth," another troublemaker named Johnson said he would whip the first preacher to stand behind the makeshift pulpit. He carried a bullwhip to accent his intentions. According to J. M. Dawson's *The Spiritual Conquest of the Southwest*, friends as well as foes of the ministers walked toward the speaker's stand. As the preachers came into view of the meeting grounds, a friend of theirs, Jesse Parker, said, "Needham, I'm glad to see you. I was afraid you wouldn't come!"

Bro. Needham Alford had his son with him, and the young man feared for his pa's safety. He interrupted the men by saying, "Pa, Mr. Johnson says the first man that goes into the stand he'll put out and cow whip."

Bacon was a slight figured man and probably did not relish a fight, but his robust friend, Alford, was quite muscular and had no fear of the hecklers. He stood his ground against the local bullies by saying, "I am able to take a whipping as any man on this ground." The opposition quietly retired, and the meeting commenced with Alford preaching first.

The troublemaker Johnson who dared the preachers to speak left the revival and mysteriously died that night. No one ever knew whether his demise was due to apoplexy or divine intervention.

Later in the revival, Bacon got his chance to expound the scriptures, but trouble raised its head once more. The alcalde sent word for him to stop preaching. Word spread from Sabine to Nacogdoches about Bacon's trouble. An extra-large crowd came to the preaching that day as his friends stood around the tabernacle daring anyone to hurt God's messenger. The sermon was delivered without a hitch.

The Presbyterian Church was not very impressed by Sumner's efforts to preach, but Rev. Benjamin Chase, a minister of that same faith, was also an agent for the American Bible Society. The paths of Sumner Bacon and Benjamin Chase crossed in Tennessee before either came to Texas, so the older man knew something about the spirit of this young preacher. Chase saw some possibilities in Bacon, even though his grammar was sorely lacking and profanity popped out of his mouth occasionally. Chase recommended Bacon as a regular agent for the American Bible Society in 1833.

Since this was the first official job the young preacher had, he was elated to be passing out the Good Book. Sumner handed the Bible to anyone willing to receive it and tackled this job with the same gusto he used in his preaching. A slight problem of defying the Mexican government's rules caused his good fortune to be shortened.

The Catholic Church looked dimly at his quest to hand out Bibles, so Bacon was arrested and became acquainted with the inside of a prison once more. This time he entered the barred cell in the town of Nacogdoches as an inmate. The authorities put him there for giving away Bibles unlawfully, although the Cumberland Presbytery in Tennessee had issued the Good Books. Bacon's actions were definitely against the law in this territory.

The preacher eventually managed his release, but horse thieves seem to follow Bacon around. At the prison in Gonzales, a father and his son were serving time for stealing horses. The jailer said, "Brother Bacon, will you pray over these two men?" He obliged, but strangely, the horse thieves decided Bacon's presence was the reason they were imprisoned. When the two were released, they did not let their coat tails touch them until they tracked down Bacon and tried to kill him. Once more Bacon was able to talk his way out of trouble.

On another occasion, Bacon passed out Bibles in the area of his old adversary, Col. Gaines. This fellow tried to stop a revival earlier, and now

Reverend Sumner Bacon, a Presbyterian minister who sold Bibles for the American Bible Society while preaching illegally in Texas. Painting by Sharon Gentry.

he wanted Bacon to quit dispersing Bibles. A Col. Bean rode up where the two men were discussing Bible distribution. Bean must have had seniority in this altercation because he told Bacon he could distribute as many Bibles as he wanted provided he didn't disturb the peace. Gaines backed down and left Bacon alone.

Bacon preached at another time in the Nacogdoches area and heard word spread that he would be arrested. Soldiers warned Bacon, so he decided to turn himself in to the authorities before they pounced on him. When he reached the commandant's office, he pleaded his case. Col. Peter Bean surprised the preacher by telling him he could expound on the scriptures all he wanted to.

Most of Bacon's time was spent in a saddle leading a packhorse loaded with Bibles. When the Almighty provided torrential rains, Sumner covered the pack with bearskins and kept plodding through the mud. However, when the rivers became swollen, they were hard for him to cross. High water forced the preacher to climb off his horse there by the river and tie both the saddle horse and pack animal. After Sumner dragged some trees into a pile, he built a log raft and floated the Bibles across while swimming the horses alongside the little boat. Then the soaking wet preacher removed the Bibles from the raft and shivered in the cold as he continued his trail through the woods of East Texas.

While Sumner delivered Bibles as a Presbyterian, David Ayres and other lay Methodists were doing the same thing. Ayres came to Texas in 1834, and his saddlebags bulged with Spanish, as well as English, Testaments that he put into eager hands. In fact, Ayres brought with him in May 1834 what he believed to be the first box of Bibles ever shipped to Texas. Unknown to Ayres, Bacon had been distributing the Good Book for a full year before Ayres got to Texas.

Ayres's early life paralleled Bacon's in that both men spent their younger years in cities on the eastern coast. Ayres and his wife were married in 1815 in the John Street Methodist Church in New York City. They established a home in Ithaca where he was a merchant and a devoted Methodist. He aided the establishment of Methodism in that area and helped build the first church. However, Ayres decided to pull up roots and make the long trip to Texas.

In 1833 Ayres left his family behind, sailed to his new home and landed off the shores of Texas. He floated up the Brazos River on a boat to a point where he planned to establish a home at Washington-on-the-Brazos, which was near present-day Navasota. For twelve months, David Ayres labored to finish a house for his brood. The following year he returned to the eastern states and brought his family and his brother with him to Texas. They settled at a temporary spot, a place on the Nueces at San Patricio. A few months later, David loaded his family, baggage and all, and took them to their stone house that he completed the previous year at Washington-on-the Brazos. Eventually the Ayres family unloaded all their belongings and set up permanent housekeeping.

David Ayres established a mercantile business in Texas similar to the company he once owned in New York. To their surprise, the Ayres family found no schools in this sparsely populated area. David and his wife, Mary, decided the best thing for them to do was to hold classes in their home with the help of Lydia Ann McHenry, who did most of the teaching. One of the rooms in their house became a makeshift classroom as they cleared away furniture and arranged tables to act as desks.

While the Ayres couple had boys and girls running in and out of their house, a neighbor made a noisy commotion of another sort. Noah T. Byers heated a forge and banged on metal in his Washington-on-the-Brazos blacksmithing shop. He could fix broken plows and wheels as well as anybody's gun because back in South Carolina, he had learned to be a gunsmith. Immediately after the Declaration of Independence from Mexico was signed in that town, Byers was appointed armorer of the Texas Army. But through the next several years, the Ayres family knew Byers only as a blacksmith and a person who repaired guns.

As people separated during the War for Independence, neighbors lost track of each other. David Ayres did not know the rest of the story about blacksmith Byers. After the battle for Texas's independence was over, Byers became the sergeant-at-arms of the Texas Senate and justice of the peace in Travis County. All these notable jobs did not surpass the new one he decided to attack. He had been a charter member of the Baptist church in Washington-on-the-Brazos before the war, so God's word was important to him. On October 16, 1841, Byers was ordained to preach that word. This thirty-three-year-old man devoted his next forty years to establishing churches in central Texas.

But as Byers and Ayres lived along the Brazos in pre-independence days, they had no way of knowing that one of their young neighbors would eventually play an important role in Texas's independence. Their lawyer friend William B. Travis also lived in Washington County during the 1830s. He knew the Ayres family quite well. Lawyer Travis was the person who settled boundary disputes, contested horse races, and other squabbles among the Texas immigrants. Travis divorced his wife after they had a son named Charles.

Travis loved his son very much and kept him as near as possible. However, his son, Charles Edward Travis, went to the Ayres School and stayed with them when his father left town and fought the Mexican soldiers. With this Methodist couple, young Charles not only learned his arithmetic and grammar but also learned Godly ways to live.

This young lawyer, William Travis, anxiously pushed for Texas to gain its freedom from Mexico. Early in the conflict, he called up some volunteer troops and led a skirmish against Mexican soldiers near Anahuac. This military post on the northeast bank of Galveston Bay protected the mouth of the Trinity River. Prisoners of the Mexican government built this fort and lighthouse in 1821, so Mexican troops fought to keep the post protected.

Saying the word "Anahuac" brought to Mexican people the memory of a large area fifty miles by thirty miles where present-day Mexico City is located. But in 1830, "Anahuac" meant an important port in Texas.

Texas leaders in the revolution soon realized they needed to control this strategic port along their coast. This location involved access to the San Jacinto and Neches Rivers, as well as the Trinity, rivers the Texans could use to transport goods and troops.

For this reason, Travis attacked the Mexican soldiers at their fort. Although Travis was captured and imprisoned at Anahuac, he later was released. He liberated that Mexican fort in the early stages of skirmishes with the Lone Star State's ruling Mexican delegation.

War looked like a sure thing, and men like Bacon and Ayres wanted to preach God's message openly. However, due to his agreement with the Mexican government, Stephen Austin opposed it. He told the religious leaders he would have to "imprison any preacher he saw that wasn't Catholic." Austin went so far as to say, "One Methodist preacher would do more mischief in his colony than a dozen horse thieves."

A bystander quickly tried to explain that Austin meant "political" mischief, but people never knew for sure what Austin had in mind. The wordy preachers presented a constant problem for their Texas leader. While Austin was helping the colonists of Texas, another leader came into the Mexican-held territory in December 1832, Sam Houston. He was ready to lend his services and his shooting ability to the cause. Texas preachers would later touch his life in a special way.

Houston wanted to throw his weight into helping the settlers in this new land because he wanted a fresh start for himself. Goodness knows he had many a setback himself leading up to this point. At the age of fourteen, Sam lost his father, so he and his mother moved from Virginia to the frontier area of Blount County, Tennessee. His older brothers helped get him a job clerking in a trader's store, but he considered keeping the books work that was too confining. This occupation did not sit well with Houston, so he ran away and lived with the Cherokee Indians for three years.

When Sam returned, he tried running a country school. This arrangement did not work very long either, so he attended a session or two of an academy at Maryville. Education helped Houston, but he enjoyed his experiences in the wild country more than in a classroom. Since he lived with the Indians a while in 1817, he was asked to help move some Cherokees to a reservation. Along the way, Houston appeared before the Secretary of War, John C. Calhoun, dressed in Indian garb, for which he was chastised. This action, as well as an inquiry into Houston's integrity, brought about Sam's resignation in 1818.

This furor about his life did not seem to faze him, and Houston was elected governor of Tennessee in 1827. He married Eliza Allen in January 1829, so at the age of thirty-six everything seemed to be coming together for Houston. However, bliss was short lived. Three months after the wedding, Eliza left him, and the governor resigned his post. In a dejected state of mind Sam Houston returned to live with the Indians.

Soon Houston made trips to Washington on behalf of his blood brothers. According to Sam, the government mistreated the Cherokee. President Andrew Jackson, realizing Houston's ability to talk with the Indians, asked him to travel to Texas in 1832 to negotiate treaties with the Indians there. This was an effort by the government to protect the white settlers coming to that area. The fact that Houston decided to stay in Texas was good for the settlers there because he immediately began to work in the constitutional convention, which met in San Felipe. His previous experience as a lawyer in Tennessee and as a governor helped him organize this new land. Houston had to turn his face the other way though, when the country preachers stood up against the Mexican government.

Many people came to Texas as Houston did for a new beginning. Two brothers, James W. and Daniel Parker, came to Texas in 1832, but each one had a different agenda. James had a wife, Patsy, and six children following him to this country to start a new home. Daniel Parker's mind dwelt on starting a Primitive Baptist Church like the one he left in Illinois. Before Daniel went many steps toward organizing a church, the

Roman Catholic Church told him in no uncertain terms there would be no church and no preaching from his Primitive Baptist text.

Daniel Parker was creative, to say the least, so he returned to Lamote, Illinois, and on July 26, 1833, organized a congregation of thirty-six members. Each member in this Pilgrim Predestinarian Regular Baptist Church was the head of a household. Parker hurried them to pack up their belongings in an oxcart and head to Texas. After quite a trip over the plains region and through the dense undergrowth of Arkansas and Louisiana, this group of thirty-six families finally saw the piney woods of East Texas.

Somehow Parker thought his group could worship safely as immigrants. Their first meeting as a church in Texas occurred inside Austin's colony on January 25, 1835. Now the group claimed the name Pilgrim Primitive Baptist Church. They later were acknowledged as the first Baptist church in Texas. Since their regular meeting day would be the Saturday before the first Sunday of the month, Daniel Parker would preach on Saturday as well as Sunday. He gave them both barrels, of religion.

Just when Daniel Parker had his people settled, another group came to Texas with a very different agenda. By April of that same year, Santa Anna was marching into Texas, and the church members had to prepare for a quick exit. One group kept the church minute book among their belongings while the church ceased to meet until the war was over. After Texas defeated the Mexican Army, Daniel Parker and Garrison Greenwood had the church's blessings to organize more churches, so they successfully started fourteen congregations in counties such as Nacogdoches, Houston, Sabine, Shelby, Liberty and Montgomery.

Parker, with limited education in his youth, never let that slow him down from preaching his belief in "Two Seedism." His theory was that since Adam's time, mankind has been born with two seeds: divine and diabolical. Daniel Parker wrote two pamphlets in 1836 to explain his beliefs: "Views on the Two Seeds" and "The Second Dose of Doctrine on the Two Seeds." His titles sounded like he thought people could be good or bad. Before leaving Illinois, he published the *Church Advocate*, a newspaper, from 1829 to 1831. Earlier in 1822, Parker served in the Illinois State Senate. Once he got to Texas, he was elected to serve also as a member of the Fourth Congress of Texas in 1839. However, he was a bit surprised when the government barred him from serving in this capacity because clergy were constitutionally ineligible in the Lone Star State.

While Daniel Parker spread God's word, his brother James Parker stirred up trouble. These two brothers had a famous niece named Cynthia Ann Parker who was captured by the Indians in 1836 along with James Parker's grandson. Cynthia became the wife of an Indian warrior and had a son, Quanah, known as a famous Comanche chief. In 1858 she was liberated by a group of soldiers and rangers who massacred an undefended Indian camp.

While James Parker searched for Cynthia, he also worked to get back his fifteen-month-old grandson, James Pratt Plummer. By 1842, the child called Tommy was ransomed through efforts of the U. S. agents and the Republic of Texas government.

Rather than bring Tommy home to his daughter's family, Uncle James Parker told his son-in-law he had paid $200 for the ransom and wanted money for the boy. This action was quite a blow, so the little boy's father wrote President Sam Houston asking for help in obtaining his child. On April 17, 1843, Houston replied that Parker had been out no expense in the transaction and for the first time Houston realized the true character of James Parker. Houston wrote the boy's father and said "he had not supposed him capable of practicing such scandalous fraud upon his kindred and connexions."

While preachers like Parker and Sumner worked for the Lord, Sam Houston planned freedom for Texas. During the months before the bullets started flying between Mexican and Texan troops, preachers secretly met their congregation in homes and continued to hand out Bibles. Every day brought a challenge of some sort for a lonely preacher like Sumner Bacon.

He fought Indians and Mexicans with his six-shooter since they did not listen to his explanations about God's love. Sumner actually wanted all Texans to feel as if they were part of God's family.

Texas always had plenty of "wild beasts" to aggravate a lone rider because bears and wolves were common. However, God was riding alongside of Bacon so he persevered. Eventually, someone mentioned to him that it might be time for him to be ordained since he had labored in Texas five years with no official credentials.

Bacon remembered that the Presbyterian Church had not looked favorably on his ordination earlier due to a little problem of no education, but a friend of his, Benjamin Chase, convinced the church leaders that Bacon needed to be ordained. The church fathers relented and set up the service to carry out the ordination in 1835. Normally this procedure took two or more days to complete all the steps for a preacher's ordination. However, Bacon was too busy to waste several days, so the church leaders took care of all steps in the service by rolling it into a one-day affair. The newly ordained Bacon left the church, saddled his horse and continued distributing Bibles that he had obtained through the American Bible Society. Over a period of two years, Bacon handed out about 2,000 Bibles that were written in both English and Spanish.

Although Bacon was a Presbyterian, he would hold revivals with ministers of other denominations. In September 1835, he and Peter Hunter Fullinwider helped two Methodist ministers hold a meeting at Caney Creek, which is near present-day Kenney. For Sumner Bacon, this meeting was a reunion of sorts. In 1830 and part of 1831, he taught school at Caney Creek.

Although several denominations had ministers in Texas, some Christians felt that more men of God were needed there. They felt that various denominational leaders needed to put forth a greater effort to send preachers to Texas. In August 1835, shortly before the war started, lawyer William Travis wrote a letter to the editor of the Methodist magazine, *Christian Advocate,* published in New York. He urged the leaders to send more preachers.

However, the winds of change were in the air, and preaching was going to have to take a back seat to fighting for Texas's independence. By late 1835, all of Texas knew war was just around the corner. As early as October 8, 1835, Sam Houston said in his departmental orders from Nacogdoches, "Our only ambition is the attainment of rational liberty—the freedom of religious opinions and just laws." Those were fighting words when heard by the ruling Mexican government.

In 1835 many fighting men like James Bowie were in Texas ready to fight the Mexican soldiers. During that year, Sumner Bacon held a revival near San Augustine. Some ruffians tried to break up the meeting, which was also visited by Colonel Bowie. According to Richard Beard in his book *Brief Biographical Sketches of Some of the Early Ministers of the*

Sumner Bacon preached under brush arbors and tabernacles similar to this one located at Sipe Springs, Texas. Author's collection.

Cumberland Presbyterian Church, Bowie told the troublemakers, "Col. Bowie is in command today." He made the sign of the cross on the ground and indicated to Bacon to continue the service.

Bowie was one of many people who now called Texas home. Along with Austin's group who rattled their wagons down the dusty Texas prairie came many other settlers who entered illegally. From 1830 to 1834, the population doubled along this frontier land. The new head-count for the Tejas country tallied about 20,000 immigrants, but the following year of 1835 saw the country's population swell in numbers as a thousand immigrants came to Texas per month. By 1836, there were twice as many immigrants as Mexican citizens, and the latter were not very happy. Austin wrote that stopping the immigrants was, "like trying to stop the Mississippi with a dam of straw."

Sumner Bacon and David Ayres came to Texas for the sole purpose of distributing Bibles and God's message. Although the Mexican authorities opposed their efforts, these two men successfully gave several thousand Bibles to Mexican and white Texans over a period of five years. The guns of war would soon blast away, but tucked inside many a soldier's pocket was a Bible to carry with him to the front lines.

2

PREACHERS FOUGHT FOR TEXAS'S INDEPENDENCE: 1836

Although many Texans worried about Spanish rule, not everybody had the same solution to the Mexican government's control of Texas. "Independence" continued to be shouted by most immigrants, so Stephen Austin finally sent letters to the mother country of Mexico. He hoped to get in their good graces and reach a compromise. Austin thought he could sit down at a meeting with Mexican leaders and work out an agreement where his people would have one part of Texas, and the Mexicans would keep the other territory. But fiery Texas leaders like Travis wanted to draw their swords and fight for independence.

When General Antonio Lopez de Santa Anna became president of Mexico, many Texan settlers felt that he would listen to their grievances. They believed he would let them separate from Mexico to become a state of their own. But Stephen Austin, electing to take the petition to Mexico stating those facts, ran into a snag. The cogs of the Mexican government moved slowly, so Mexican officials did not jump to reply to the settlers' request. After waiting a long time, Austin sent them a blunt letter outlining what he would do, if they did not let Texans have their independence.

When his letter fell into the wrong hands, Austin suddenly looked down Mexican soldiers' gun barrels. They slapped the Texas leader into a Mexican jail for eighteen months while Santa Anna prepared to send an army to Texas. By the time Austin walked out of his cell and returned to Texas in 1835, he knew war was the only solution for his countrymen.

When the war started in the fall of 1835, Sumner Bacon searched other places to fund his Bible distribution project. The Texas colonists had no extra money to spend on the Good Book when guns and gunpowder came first. Bacon was acquainted with many southerners because of extensive travels he made as a young man among the cotton fields and cypress trees. On this trip, he talked with plantation owners in Louisiana, Mississippi and Tennessee as he raised cash for Bibles.

At Spring Hill, Tennessee, Sumner Bacon's interest deviated from cash and turned to a pretty southern belle named Elizabeth McKerall. By the following January, Sumner Bacon and Elizabeth married. He brought his new bride from her home in Tennessee all the way to San Augustine, Texas. After such a long trip, some newlyweds would set up housekeeping and "sit a spell." However, Sumner hardly let his coattail settle before he left his bride with Rev. Samuel McMahon's household in San Augustine.

The Texas Revolution was in full swing, and he aimed to be a part of it. He joined the Texas troops as a chaplain and as a courier for Sam Houston. While Bacon prepared for war, other preachers such as George Slaughter attempted to spread the gospel without getting caught.

Slaughter, born in Mississippi May 10, 1811, moved with his parents in 1824 to Louisiana where George received his complete education, three weeks of school. By 1830 the Slaughter family crossed the Sabine River and ushered themselves in as citizens of the Mexican State of Coahuila and Texas. The new Texans soon discovered that the Mexican petty officers did not allow any religious freedom.

Several Protestant clergymen found themselves in jail thanks to arrests by a Mexican, Col. Jose de las Piedras. George Slaughter was about nineteen years old when the colonists first tried to reason with the Mexicans to release the preachers. When the jail guards refused to give up the parsons, the Texans opened fire, killed several Mexicans and removed their friends from behind bars. Slaughter saw his first action against the Mexican soldiers as he fired on Col. Piedras's men.

Slaughter rolled his freight wagons between Louisiana and Texas while the colonists made plans to revolt against the Mexican government. At this time, George was preaching on Sundays while he freighted cargo the other six days. During his visit to court in Natchitoches, Louisiana, Slaughter talked with Sam Houston who was dressed in Indian garments, complete with feathers and silver ornaments. After Slaughter discussed his job as a freighter with Sam Houston, the white-skinned Indian gave the young man a job. George Slaughter was hired to carry messages and haul supplies in his wagons to the Texas troops.

When Houston moved from one town to another, he had a large legal library that he carried with him. He asked Slaughter to carry this extensive set of books to Nacogdoches. The freighter was happy to oblige this great leader of Texas, so he hitched up his team of horses to his wagon to carry Houston's library. As men watched Slaughter hauling Houston's belongings, most of them would have agreed that the freighter was on good terms with the Texas leader.

Slaughter was in for a surprise. The Mexican authorities learned that the teamster named George Slaughter often stood before a pulpit somewhere along the trail and preached in a Protestant gathering rather than remaining on the wagon seat as a freighter. Mexican troops ushered Slaughter into a jail cell for this offense, and Houston did not intercede to get him out. While Slaughter cooled his heels in a cell, the war between the Mexican troops and the Texans became more intense. Men like Col. William Travis knew they were in for a fierce showdown soon, so he returned to the David Ayres family to see his son Charles once more before the war escalated. The little boy was seven years old at the time.

Finally, talkative George Slaughter managed to convince the sheriff to open the jail doors to his cell in time for him to fight with Sam Houston's troops. The Texas soldiers marched toward Goliad and stopped on high ground to watch the huge army of Santa Anna approaching the Alamo. Everyone positioned on the hillside could see Santa Anna's masses. They marched forward with so many troops that they looked like a huge swarm of ants from a distance.

At this time, men could go and come through the Alamo gates, so Houston told Slaughter to give the Alamo soldiers orders to retreat. The freighter maneuvered through the area without the Mexican soldiers catching him. Once inside the Alamo's walls, Slaughter pleaded with Travis, Bowie and Crockett as he explained Houston's command for them to retreat. But the order fell on deaf ears. These men held their ground, determined to defend the old mission.

Slaughter gave the people remaining in the old mission the only encouragement he knew. The parson read from the Holy Bible and prayed for the courageous soldiers. After preaching to these men, Slaughter quietly slipped out of the Alamo and returned to his wagon.

According to some accounts, shortly after the freighter left the Alamo, Travis drew his famous line in the dirt as he asked each man to walk to his side of the line, if he would die for Texas's independence. Colonel William Barrett Travis was a forceful speaker as he eloquently extolled the virtues of fighting for Texas and dying for Texas on that March 3, 1836. One by one the soldiers inside the old mission walked across the line, all except Moses Rose.

After fighting for ten days inside the confines of the old mission, Moses decided on a new plan of action. According to Frank Tolbert's book, *An Informal History of Texas,* Rose said, "I am not prepared to die and shall not do so if I can avoid it." He slipped over the wall, traveled through enemy territory and eluded the Mexican troops.

While the men at the Alamo stood their ground against the Mexican troops, many civilians left their homes to flee from the Mexican soldiers. David Ayres and his family lived in the path of Santa Anna's advancing army, so they burned all the buildings around their house. They could not bear the thought of Mexican troops eating their food and sleeping in their beds. Hurriedly the Ayres family took a box of Bibles, clothes, and food with them where they lived in the woods for almost three months. Ayres moved his wife and children from time to time as they avoided the oncoming soldiers.

This act of fleeing from the Mexican army was called the "Runaway Scrape." William Travis's son, Charles, accompanied the Ayres family in their flight from the Mexican troops. While the Ayres family ran for their lives, Travis and others gave their lives for the cause in the early morning hours of March 6, 1836. Little Charles Travis was told about his father's death while he was running to save his own skin.

While some Texans ran away from the battles, others did what they could to help Texas's cause. One day Sumner Bacon returned to Gen. Sam Houston's camp after taking dispatches to his troops. Houston instructed Bacon to make a quick trip to New Orleans to buy $561 of cannon powder for the troops. As the parson prepared to leave, Sam Houston said, "Now Bro. Bacon—long rides and short prayers." When Bacon purchased the gunpowder, he paid for it with his own money.

The preacher's next trip involved a visit to General Dunlap of Tennessee to ask his help in fighting the Mexican invasion, which Houston expected soon. Since Bacon spent a lot of time in the saddle as he moved through the Southern states a decade before, he may have met the Dunlap family on an earlier trip to that area.

While Bacon ran errands for Sam Houston, other preachers fought in the War for Independence. Rev. John Wesley Kenney served in the Texas Army from September 11, 1835, until April 21, 1836. His unit fought at San Jacinto, but he missed that battle because he was on a two-week furlough helping his family escape from the Mexican Army. Kenney met David Ayres at a conference in early September of 1835, where a group of Texas preachers voted to ask the Missionary Society of the Methodist Episcopal Church to send missionaries to Texas. Ayres was secretary of this meeting. At that time, Kenney was asked to take pastoral charge of all Methodist work west of the Trinity River. The war interrupted all their plans for a while.

John Wesley Kenney, with his family, arrived in Texas in 1833, and built the initial cabin that would later be part of the town called Washington-on-the-Brazos. The parson saddled his horse and visited people up the river to Gay Hill and down the Brazos River to San Felipe, Columbia and Brazoria. The following year, 1834, Kenney preached on Caney Creek, the first camp meeting in Texas west of the Trinity River. All of this traveling did not keep the man busy enough, so he worked as a surveyor for Austin's colony part of the time.

Meanwhile, Bacon acted as a carrier for San Houston in 1836. He delivered messages to the Alamo, to Goliad and to Victoria. His Bibles turned up in unusual places.

Washington H. Secrest, a scout with Erastus "Deaf" Smith, discovered one of Bacon's Bibles in a strange set of events. Secrest was present when Santa Anna's troops moved toward San Felipe de Austin. This town of six hundred inhabitants was on the western bank of the Brazos River.

San Felipe de Austin was the hub of the Revolution because it served as the headquarters of Austin's colony. By the time Santa Anna's troops made their way across Texas, at least three steamboats made regular runs from the coast up to San Felipe with goods as they navigated the Brazos River. As long as steamboats paddled up the river, stores had cloth, plows and other goods to sell. Some early conventions of the Texans in 1832 and 1833 were held in this town, so it was recognized as a position of importance in the early years of the state's life.

Scouts informed Moseley Baker, leader of the garrison in San Felipe, of Santa Anna's approaching army. Baker tried to protect this town of San Felipe de Austin, which was about two miles from present-day Sealy. He wanted to keep the Mexican troops from crossing the Brazos River, so his soldiers gallantly held their position as the gunfire raged. Mexican troops fought relentlessly.

After several days of fighting, messengers finally convinced Baker that he must evacuate the town, so he readied the inhabitants for the inevitable—the town must be burned. He told the people that each person could pick something out of the rabble before the torch was lit to burn everything in sight.

Washington Secrest, a Texas scout, rummaged among the stacks of household items as he looked for something of value. He found a small Bible that once belonged to Sumner Bacon and selected it as his "spoils of battle." Years later he joined the Methodist Church at Ruterville and told the congregation that he read the little Bible every day since the burning of San Felipe.

The War for Independence changed the life of men in different ways. Washington Secrest left San Felipe and fought in the battle of San Jacinto. He and five other soldiers broke through enemy lines and pointed their rifles at none other than Santa Anna himself. With his capture came the turning of the tide. The Texans won the battle. While fighting against the Mexicans, Washington Secrest received a bullet aimed at his chest. The Bible in his breast pocket stopped the shell. That same Bible he picked up in the streets of San Felipe saved his life. This experience changed his feelings about God for all times to come. He became a Christian.

Rev. Hugh Martin Childress fought in the Battle of San Jacinto also. He was known as the "Bear Hunter Preacher," so he had his sights on his gun well adjusted for the shooting that occurred against the Mexican troops. While Childress was hunting, he must have run into Noah Smithwick, a blacksmith who repaired guns for the Texas soldiers during their battle with the Mexican Army. Noah understood Spanish and was an interpreter-agent with Plains Indians seeking treaties and trading posts. He actually lived with a tribe of Comanches for a period of time.

Smithwick said Childress was a fine preacher, the kind that the frontier wanted. Noah Smithwick, in his book *The Evolution of a State, or Recollections of Old Texas Days,* complimented Rev. Childress:

Major Movements of Texas and Mexican Military Forces, February–April, 1836. Courtesy of the General Libraries, the University of Texas at Austin.

"He was an expert with a violin, and even 'tripped the light fantastic.' For an all around useful man he had few equals, always bearing his full share of anything, from a prayer meeting to an Indian fight."

Childress and Washington Secrest were not the only men who fought in the San Jacinto battle and lived to talk about God and religion. Matthew Walter, a physician and Disciples of Christ minister, treated the wounded Sam Houston at the time that soldiers brought Santa Anna to him. Walter served as a surgeon during the War for Independence and as a representative for Red River County when the First Texas Congress convened. Walter continued to preach, ranch and doctor sick people for the next twenty years.

When the Mexican War started, Walter signed up with Company F of the Texas Rifles. This preacher never let his horse get out of a lather because he was either driving his cattle to greener grass, serving at a political convention or preaching. A short time before the Civil War commenced, Walter drove a large herd of cattle across Texas with other families. They grazed North Texas in the summer and wintered in Central Texas. This arrangement allowed the preacher to speak to many different people.

Walter had a strange thing happen to him in 1864: A vigilante group arrested him as a Union sympathizer. They promptly put him in the Gainesville jail. This predicament was very dangerous because Matthew Walter knew of previous hangings performed by the same vigilante group. The preacher contacted a fellow Mason, Capt. Ephraim M. Daggett, for help and fortunately was released.

Just as Matthew Walter moved on to other activities after the War for Texas's Independence, George Slaughter, freighter to Houston, did likewise. He had more than one reason to be happy about the Texas victory. Now that the state could proclaim itself a republic, Protestant marriages were legal for the first time. George often found himself on the doorstep of the Mason house where he courted Sarah. The preacher and Miss Mason were in love. Somehow between the victory at San Jacinto and other skirmishes, George obtained permission to go home and marry her.

When Texas won its independence, preachers flowed into the Republic at a rapid pace. These travelers needed information, so John Wesley Kenney's house acted as the first stop for some Methodist clergy coming to Texas on their initial trip. In 1837, Kenney played host to Methodists missionaries like Robert Alexander, Littleton Fowler and Martin Rutger.

As more preachers came to the area, older preachers like Kenney reduced their loads. He graced the pulpit only on weekends and held one or two camp meetings a year.

In 1838, the preacher's brother, Thomas, was murdered at Kenney's Fort near Round Rock. The parson's family realized that the Kenney children had no parents, so these three babies became a part of their own family of two boys and a daughter. He and his wife adopted the children and raised them.

Just a short time after Texas enjoyed its new freedom from Mexico, settlers wanted land held by agricultural tribes like the Cherokee Indians. Sam Houston cared for these Native Americans who loved to till the rich East Texas soil, so he negotiated a treaty with them February 25, 1836. Members of the Texas Senate of 1837 did not share Houston's concern for the Indians and failed to ratify the agreement.

When Houston left office, his successors dealt harshly with the Cherokee people with proclamations demanding the Indians leave their farms. This normally peaceful tribe felt that it was being asked to do the impossible. By 1839 the Indians staged an uprising that caused bloodshed. George Slaughter became a captain for a company of soldiers organized in Sabine. They traveled to reinforce General Rusk who had a small group of soldiers camped on the Neches River. Nearby Chief Bowles had 1,600 Cherokees prepared for battle.

Two days of exasperating truce talks proved nothing, so Rusk led his men against the Indians. When the battle cries ended, the Cherokees lost eleven braves and Rusk lost only three men. A second battle commenced between the Indians and the soldiers. When gunfire ceased this time, the Indians had lost over a hundred warriors including Chief Bowles. The Indians fled after this defeat, but Captains Slaughter and Todd followed them to ensure they retreated all the way to the Trinity River.

Now the preacher-cowboy, George Slaughter, who worked so long for Sam Houston and Texas, could turn his energy toward his family and making a living. In 1852, he moved all his possessions, lock, stock, and barrel, to Freestone County. His ninety-two head of cattle grazing near the old town of Butler found plenty of green grass. Cattle multiplied under these conditions, and Slaughter counted 600 head in his herd within five short years.

People in his area kept hearing glorious stories about the big ranches in the western part of Texas. The Slaughters also heard about these open spaces where everyone could homestead a spread, so they packed up their belongings again to see if this was true. Their wagons rolled toward Comanche County for a stop. After living there for a while, George Slaughter eventually made his way to Palo Pinto County for new adventures.

While Slaughter moved westward, Bacon returned to his wife who had been staying with Samuel McMahon in San Augustine for the duration of the war. Bacon purchased two hundred acres of land for $750 six miles east of San Augustine. After he had a place for his family to live, Bacon set about finishing his lifelong dream.

He organized the first Cumberland Presbyterian Church in Texas in the summer of 1836. His next order of business was to organize a Presbytery, a regional organization of ministers in Texas. He traveled to Mississippi to get permission to do this by asking the Synod. As soon as he had three or more Presbyterian ministers in Texas, his dream would come true. He waited a year before the required number of preachers called the Republic of Texas their home. Then he convened a meeting at his home November 27, 1837, and the Presbytery of Texas became a reality.

His health became so bad that he could preach only once a month, so he became an inactive minister in 1838. Bacon spent more time with his family on the farm. He died in 1844, and was buried in Chapel Hill Cemetery only five miles east of San Augustine. This town was always home to him and his wife for their short numbers of years spent together. Sumner Bacon succeeded in scattering many Bibles over his beloved Texas while helping her win independence.

As Texans celebrated their independence from Mexico, they thought life would be rather serene in the new Republic. Preachers like Sumner and Slaughter crisscrossed the state telling the "Good News," so evil men would be converted. For many years prior to the War for Independence, Mexican priests visited their citizens as well as the Indians in Texas.

Texans living near the Gulf of Mexico had to worry about their safety from the native warriors. In 1840 most people living in Linnville probably made their living fishing in nearby Lavaca Bay. Major Watts tended the customs office situated a few miles out of Linnville. Suddenly Comanche Indians appeared from nowhere on a hot August day and raided Watts's office. They killed and scalped him. Next the warriors grabbed his wife and tore off her outer clothing. With intent to rape her, they yanked at her corset, but the tight material would not give. No matter how much they pulled on the fabric, it refused to stretch. By this time the rest of the town was alerted to the invasion and jumped into their boats and paddled away.

When the Indians became quite exasperated with the girdle, they tied Mrs. Watts to a tree, shot an arrow into her breast and left the customs office. By the time the raiding party rode down the streets of Linnville screaming a battle cry, the town was deserted. While taking time with Mrs. Watts's girdle, the Indians had given the citizens just long enough to paddle their boats across the bay to safety. When the warriors disappeared, the Texas Militia found Mrs. Watts. The corset saved not only her virtue but also her life. She survived the ordeal with only a sunburn and slight wound to show for her experience. Linnville residents could say they were the town "saved by a girdle."

What time Texans were not fighting Indians or plowing their crops, their hearts turned to God. Well into the 1850s, revival meetings continued where several denominations met to sing and pray under tabernacles or in churches. In Waco in 1854, such a revival took place where the preachers tallied the converts after the final service ended. The Methodists received sixty-one members to the Baptists' forty-two. This section of Texas was an area that the Methodists organized earlier than the Baptists, but they admitted the Baptists were coming along in numbers. In fact, J. M. Dawson once said, "If the Baptists got to a new community before the Methodists, they had to go in on the cowcatcher of the first train."

Life after the War for Independence was better for a great number of people but worse for others. One example was Texan Charles Travis who had a strong leader as a father but did not have a very productive life himself. Although William Travis's decision to leave Charles with David Ayres is known, few Texans knew the story about the little boy's mother.

Rosanna Travis divorced William in November of 1835 and married Dr. Samuel B. Cloud in New Orleans on February 15, 1836. Dr. Cloud was a successful doctor as well as planter. The wedding took place less than three weeks before William Travis died in the Alamo. However, his son Charles Travis was already on Texas soil. Months earlier Rosanna allowed Travis to come into their home and take little Charlie to Texas. Since his father was dashing about from one battle to another as he fought the Mexican army, this six-year-old boy was placed in the care of David Ayres.

In a diary that William Travis gave to his law partner Franklin Jefferson Starr, a Texas woman, Miss Mary Elizabeth Cummins, was mentioned.

She was thought to be the daughter of Judge Moses Cummins, a lawyer and surveyor who traveled to Texas with Austin's first group of immigrants. Some interpretations of the diary suggest that William Travis and Mary Elizabeth were in love.

This diary would have been destroyed in the burning of San Felipe de Austin, except that Travis's friend, Franklin Starr went on a furlough to take his family to safety. For some unknown reason, Travis gave Franklin his diary earlier and included other papers.

On February 24, 1836, William Travis wrote a valiant plea for help as he stood with his men inside the Alamo. He ended the stirring letter by saying, "Victory or Death." Before this letter was given to a carrier, he also scribbled a note to David Ayres on a dirty piece of wrapping paper, which said, "Take care of my little boy. If the country should be saved, I may make him a splendid fortune; but if the country is lost and I should perish, he will have nothing but the proud recollection that he is the son of a man who died for his country."

After William Travis died in the Alamo, Charles Travis stayed two more years with the David Ayres family; then he returned to his mother's home as a twelve-year-old. Charles stayed in New Orleans until both his mother and stepdad died of a fever epidemic in 1848. At that time, he returned to Texas and lived a while with his sister, Susan Isabelle, in Brenham. Their father supposedly left them a sizable amount of land upon his death. His will explained that his two children were to "share and share alike." Charles Travis followed in his lawyer-father's footsteps when he earned a law degree from Baylor University at Waco.

David Ayres and his wife raised Charles Travis in their Christian home, so the Ayres family felt proud when Charles Travis ran for the Texas Legislature and won. He served in this capacity during the 1853-1854 term representing Caldwell and Hays counties. The biblical principles they taught him seemed to be working early in his life, but Charles eventually took a different direction.

Charlie became bored with government and decided to serve as a Texas Ranger. He had the title of Captain in Company E of the Second U.S. Cavalry in 1854, which was stationed at Fort Clark. This area of Texas, full of open spaces and cacti, must not have agreed with him. Charles probably became restless because he soon headed his saddle horse to Missouri. He accepted the title of Captain in the Second U.S. Cavalry there March 5, 1855.

At that time Charles served with Colonel Albert Sidney Johnston and the cavalry. One time this particular group of soldiers found themselves on a long march to Texas. Charles and his men were to protect Texas from the lawless element that ranged along the Rio Grande.

But Charles Travis did not fare very well while returning to the Lone Star State. Several charges of misconduct were brought against him. Charles stood before a military court in Fort Mason in 1856. This particular fort directed all operations in that part of Texas so his case appeared on their docket. The court presented charges against Captain Charles Travis, which included slander, cheating at cards, and unauthorized absence from camp. Charles' behavior was stated as "conduct unbecoming an officer and a gentleman." When the court reached a decision, it was a "guilty" verdict against this son of Texas's hero, William Travis.

Charles Travis did not take the findings of the court sitting down. He fought the charges and tried to get the men who testified against him to recant, but they refused. No matter how Travis tried to convince them to change their story, they held strong to their version of the events. He even appealed the decision of the court to United States President Franklin Pierce, but public opinion went against him, and the president refused to reopen the case. Travis became a dejected man and died of consumption at his sister's house in Washington County. He was only thirty-one years of age when he was buried at Chappell Hill in 1860.

Although Charles Travis's story ended, the David Ayres family who helped to raise him, continued to aid the Christian cause in Texas. In the fall of 1842, a young Methodist minister named Homer Spellman Thrall landed in Galveston and preached his first sermon on Texas soil at the Ryland Chapel. Soon his path crossed with that of David Ayres. The older man of God took the young fellow under his wing, and at Bastrop they enjoyed the Texas Methodist Conference together. Soon afterward, Thrall was listed as a Methodist circuit rider that preached in homes and at camp meetings.

Homer Thrall got to Texas in time to see plenty of Indians. In 1844 he preached the first camp meeting in the area of modern-day Cuero on the Guadalupe River. Indian raids were so common along the river that

Thrall had to preach with gun-toting help. Texas Rangers stood around the brush arbor while he preached.

By 1846 this preacher from Vermont was sent to work in the Austin circuit. This opportunity gave Thrall a chance to preach to generals, governors and chief justices. He finally was able to see the completed construction of a Methodist church in Austin, debt free. Thrall rode the Washington circuit in 1848-1849 and helped organize the successful Methodist paper called the *Texas Wesleyan Banner.* Rev. Thrall also found time to be a teacher. College professors did not live very cloistered lives in the early days. Thrall would find himself in front of a class teaching at Rutersville College one day then riding horseback over long stretches of countryside the next day as a circuit rider.

Thrall felt a long way from his home of Vermont, but when the Civil War started, he took not the side of his Northern family but the side of his new Texas friends. Whereas the northern Methodist churches openly preached against slavery, Thrall agreed with his Texas neighbors' feelings, so he became a part of the Methodist Episcopal Church. This congregation was more lenient on slave owners than the northern Methodists, of which Texas had plenty.

Thrall continued to preach, teach and write books. He had a busy pen as he completed *History of Methodism* in 1872, *A History of Texas* in 1876, *A Pictorial History of Texas* in 1879, *The People's Illustrated Almanac, Texas Handbook, and Immigrants' Guide* in 1880 and *A Brief History of Methodism in Texas* in 1889.

While Thrall kept his pen busy, George Slaughter and other circuit riders continued to preach the good news. Many people were influenced by the circuit riders they met even though their conversion took awhile. As Slaughter drove his freight wagon for Sam Houston, he may have spoken to Houston about God, but the General was not receptive to the Holy Book or the Christian life during Texas's War for Independence.

After Houston orchestrated Texas's fight to govern itself, he stayed around to help the new state grow. He won two terms as president of the Republic of Texas and held the title of U.S. Senator from Texas for fourteen years.

Houston's interest in religion up to this point depended largely on the circumstances at the time. He was first baptized into the Catholic Church in Texas when he came to the territory. Houston followed through with this ceremony so he could be a citizen and hold office under the Mexican government. On his birthday in 1836, Sam Houston made another big decision when he signed the Declaration of Independence at Washington-on-the-Brazos in March of that year.

Houston's decision to become a Christian did not happen until he was sixty-three years old. When he walked into the river with the preacher to be baptized, Houston said that people downstream better be careful. He referred to the massive amount of sins that would float down their direction when he let them go in baptism.

After that change in his heart, he tried to make every church service in his home congregation. The old statesman would sometimes be

Sam Houston led Texas troops to victory in the War for Independence. Preachers like George Slaughter and Sumner Bacon worked for him during the revolution. Courtesy of the West Texas Collection at Angelo State University, San Angelo, Texas.

a little late and come in the door while the services were already in progress. A friend, Alexander W. Terrell, explained that when he was late, Houston would slip into the last pew in the church, which was occupied by slaves. On one occasion, Houston knelt beside a young Negro boy when it was time for the congregation to pray. In that same Baptist church in Independence, Texas, in 1852 Houston predicted that the Civil War would commence in 1860 and would be a tragic event. He respected the Negroes and emphasized that they should be freed. He just did not want war.

Sam Houston was inactive during the Civil War, for he resigned his post as Governor of Texas rather than recite an oath of allegiance to the Confederacy. His vision was to see Texas independent of other governments rather than mired in the quicksand of a Civil War. Houston, who led the Republic of Texas so heroically died while the guns of the Civil War were sounding, July 26, 1863.

Other Texas circuit riders responded to the call of the Civil War and served with Bible in one hand and a gun in the other. They continued the attitude Texas preachers had during the Texas Revolutionary War. They would pray for the soldiers the best they could before the fighting started and then grab a rifle and shoot at the enemy when the guns roared. One such preacher was Bro. McGary.

When Isaac and Elizabeth McGary looked at their newly born son, Austin, on February 2, 1846, they had no idea how versatile this little boy would become. The family enjoyed the green countryside around Huntsville where God made enough rain to have bountiful crops. The Church of Christ congregation was active, and the preaching that took place inside the church's walls influenced little Austin. Three preacher brothers, Benton, Thomas and Basil Sweeny, also impressed him as they prayed to the Almighty and led their congregations in Bible study.

Austin McGary became acquainted with guns as a youngster, a trait that helped in later years. He joined the Confederate Army with his good friends Addison and Randolph Clark. During this time he followed the leadership of Sam Houston, Jr., in the Huntsville Grays.

McGary must have proven himself as a leader of men because he ran for the office of sheriff in the nearby county of Madison in 1872 and won. This job exposed him to some rough characters, but he never backed down. After serving almost two terms as sheriff, McGary admitted to a friend that he neither owned a gun nor used one. When asked why he did not have a weapon, McGary explained that his strong Christian faith made him feel that he should not bear arms against anybody.

McGary left the sheriff's job only to take on a more dangerous occupation. He delivered condemned prisoners and desperados to Texas State Penitentiary at Huntsville. Many of these convicts had nothing to lose, so when they noticed their guard had no rifle, it looked like they would have overpowered him. However, Austin McGary said, "In the two years I worked for the state, I never lost a man."

People asked McGary how he kept his prisoners. He would explain, "I am a Christian and I have the best two-barreled weapon: the Old Testament and the New Testament."

In 1881 this thirty-five-year-old man joined the Church of Christ and put up his lawman's badge. He began preaching full time and moved to Austin a couple of years later to preach in that town. He always had an ear for what was happening around the state, so it was not unusual that he attended a state meeting of representatives of the Church of Christ in Bryan. This get-together took place in June 1884.

Now that the Church of Christ minister had a permanent job where he was not moving prisoners around the country, his mind turned to matrimony. Austin McGary married Narcissus Jenkins in 1866, and they eventually had two children.

McGary felt that his denomination needed a newspaper to circulate information, so he started the *Firm Foundation* in September 1884. In his first edition he described his plans: "To oppose everything in the work and worship of the church for which there was not a command or an apostolic example or a necessary scriptural inference." Probably Church of Christ preachers, as well as members, grabbed each edition to see what was new. Editor McGary liked to expose the latest controversy in the news, and this tendency provided him with a large readership.

Finally, McGary decided to leave Texas and explore California and Oregon. Another writer took over his newspaper for a time, but McGary eventually returned to the Lone Star State. He could not keep quiet concerning the written word, so he printed two periodicals: *The Lookout* and *The Open Arena*.

McGary lost his wife after only six years of marriage. In 1875 he married Lucie Kitrell, and they had nine children. Austin McGary became a widower for the second time when Lucie died. At fifty-one, McGary married Lillian Otney, who would be his last wife. Bro. McGary, who wore many different hats in his lifetime, died in Houston at eighty-two in 1928.

Texas ministers helped their neighbors through the War of Independence as well as the Civil War and watched Texas grow as a state. As the frontier moved westward, settlers were anxious to homestead land in West Texas and the Panhandle region. Along with their wagons came circuit riders such as Rev. Andrew Jackson Potter who could ride a racehorse or punch cattle up the Kansas trail as well as preach a hellfire and brimstone message.

3

REVEREND POTTER,
FIGHTIN' JACK: 1830–1895

R ev. Andrew Jackson Potter, a West Texas circuit rider, toted a gun
and held his own with the roughest of characters. Born on April 5,
1830 in Chariton County, Missouri, to Joshua and Martha Potter, Andrew had a special namesake. Since his father fought in the War of 1812
and admired "Old Hickory" so much, he named his young son Andrew
Jackson. But this proud father did not get to watch his young son grow
into a teenager, as he died when Andrew was only ten years old. The
Jackson family of three other brothers and three sisters soon found themselves traveling about the countryside with no real home. With his family unit fragmented, Andrew Jackson slipped into the orphan category
rather quickly.

In his survival mode of existence, Andrew developed a pugnacious,
aggressive disposition on the Western frontier. He had to be that way to
live with the man for whom he worked, a character known to gamble,
race horses and drink whiskey. Since Andrew was a small boy, his mentor decided he would make a great jockey. Potter climbed aboard whatever horseflesh had a saddle while his boss carried him to horse races all
over the Southwest. Potter rode to victory in a lot of contests and probably learned to leave a town quickly when he defeated the area's best
horse. As he moved from town to town, Andrew Potter traveled the
mountains and the deserts from St. Louis to Santa Fe.

Along the way, Andrew acquired the ability to gamble and drink,
but his most useful lessons involved a gun and a pen. Between races his
mentor taught him how to draw a bead on any adversary and how to
write well enough to get by in the frontier world.

When Andrew grew into a strapping sixteen-year-old, he decided to
strike out on his own. He joined Captain Slack's company of volunteers

who fought in the Mexican War around 1846. During this period of his life, Jackson Potter learned to whip a team of oxen down the road as well as fight any Indians or Mexican troops that blocked his path.

While Potter fought against the Mexican troops, he might have noticed blonde-haired soldiers in the enemies' military forces. Americans were known occasionally to defect to the other side, but this war was different. So many Americans switched sides and joined forces with the soldiers south of the border that they formed their own Mexican-American Brigade. The United States annexed Texas, but many people opposed this action or they had other bones to pick with the U. S. government. The Mexican-American War gave these dissatisfied men a chance to vent their anger.

Mexican General Pedro de Ampudia easily lured U. S. citizens into his army. He promised them large land grants, Mexican citizenship and rapid promotion in his army. In the first few months of the war, few of the defected soldiers saw combat. Only when a Mexican trooper fell in a skirmish, would the Mexican general replace him with an American soldier. As the war progressed, more Americans joined their ranks. Eventually, they formed the San Patricio Brigade, which had three artillery companies. This group of several hundred Americans fought hard for the Mexicans and injured many U. S. soldiers.

When the American army won the battle at Churubusco in 1857, they decided it was time to discipline the American turncoats they captured. The defectors were court-martialed on charges of treason and desertion. These fellow Americans were sentenced to be hanged or to occupy hard-labor prisons where the soldiers shaved their heads and branded their cheek with a "D." In spite of this treatment, other Americans joined the San Patricio Brigade, which was not disbanded until the peace treaty between Mexico and the United States was signed in May 1848.

While deserters ran into trouble, tall, gangly Jackson Potter continued to fight on the side of the United States. Potter seemed to appear wherever a battle was brewing. He served five years with his company, which was under the command of Col. Sterling Price. The Colonel put together a group of scouts that traveled from El Paso toward Chichuachua ahead of the American forces fighting in the Mexican War.

During his first few days in the military, Potter discovered he was too small to carry a haversack and musket, not to mention being too small to tolerate the fatigue such a walk produced. For that reason, Potter became a teamster and drove ox carts to Santa Fe when the troops visited that community. Along the way, young Potter often shot at Indians and Mexicans who attacked them, but he had a compassionate side, too. He ministered to wounded soldiers as a nurse both at Santa Fe in New Mexico and at Fort Leavenworth, Kansas.

In September 1846, Potter decided to leave the hospital job and travel with the army. Still driving oxen, he left Leavenworth, Kansas, on the way to Arkansas. The regiment's destination was Bent's Fort, but on the way Cheyenne Indians attacked the train of 40 wagons. Potter and the other drivers fired at the circling warriors while trying to control their team. Too many Indians attacked the wagon train. After a short skirmish, all the wagons were captured.

This tragedy happened because the soldiers did not stay with the wagon train. Their military escort thought all was well as the wagons traveled in the area of friendly Indians, so they moved ahead of the train and were out of sight. Drivers like Potter were alone when the attack took place.

On another confrontation with Indians, the warriors used a deceptive maneuver to gain control of the freighters. Early in the morning two Indians approached the wagons and gave the sign of friendship. The cook fed them and they stayed with the train. As the oxen began their day's journey, two more warriors appeared. A larger group of friendly Indians visited with the teamsters next, and all was well until 300 warriors suddenly appeared. The Chief said he did not want their scalps, only the provisions in the wagons.

The wagon master stopped the train and handed food to the Indians. Suddenly a cloud of dust appeared on the horizon, and the teamsters yelled, "Soldiers! The soldiers are coming." The warriors disappeared, and the freighters were relieved even if the dust brought only another wagon train instead of soldiers.

On one such trip across the country, Andrew Potter's unit at Bent's Fort decided it was time to ride the three hundred miles to Santa Fe. This long journey in the winter took a lot out of the men, but they arrived at the capital town of the New Mexico Territory in January 1847.

Texas Frontier Development, 1841–1843, showing trips that Jackson Potter took to Santa Fe and Bent's Fort while serving in the U. S. Army. Courtesy of The General Libraries, The University of Texas at Austin.

This location was amid the campgrounds of the fierce Apaches. These warriors constantly harassed the soldiers as they attacked the men in blue whether they were in New Mexico or Arizona. Indians knew no territorial boundaries.

When Potter's regiment got to Santa Fe, they found many soldiers in the army hospital ward moaning as they suffered from scurvy, measles and pneumonia. Jackson Potter rolled up his sleeves and became a nurse again among the sick. He listened to their cries of delirious efforts to leave their beds. As he quieted some of the sick men, another one would yell, "Good-bye, I am going home." Potter's commander decided to load the sick in wagons and head the oxen toward the army hospital at Fort Leavenworth. Potter traveled that agonizing trip with the sick. They stopped often to bury the dead.

After six years as a soldier, Jackson decided to head to Texas as a civilian, and he reached San Antonio by 1852. Potter had a brother who lived on York's Creek in Hays County, Texas, so he planned to pay him a visit. But Potter was exposed to typhoid fever while on this trip and nearly died. Although this stout lad survived years of battle unharmed, the fever almost finished him. After months of sickness, he survived only to find himself deep in debt from the expense of the doctor's calls. Once Jackson gained his strength back, his first job was that of ox team driver. He made the whopping salary of $15 a month and eventually worked for any man who would hire him, so he could wipe the slate clean of debts.

While living with his brother, Jackson heard the gospel preached by a Methodist minister, I. G. John. The first sermon Jackson remembered hearing was John's text, "Who Is the Wise Man?" Potter returned to hear several more sermons from John. Jackson actually missed his favorite Sunday horse races so he could hear this preacher.

Jackson Potter was always looking for adventure, so even though the Lord was working on him, he turned his back on Texas to prospect for gold in California. Stories of instant millionaires in the gold field enticed Potter to seek his fortune. He endured the long hours of digging for gold in the Santa Rita mine, only to find that men like him were not destined to become rich. Very little of the shiny gold found its way into his pocket. Within a year, the young Texan was so discouraged that he decided to seek his fortunes in more familiar territory. In 1852 Potter found that freighting around San Antonio was a job he could manage.

By 1853, Potter met a Texas lady to his liking. He married Emily C. Guin of Bastrop on August 25, 1853, and intended to continue the life of a cowboy and freighter, a life he enjoyed. But Potter hauled some lumber to Bastrop in 1856 and noticed a camp meeting was in progress. Jackson remembered preacher John's words that spoke to him along York's Creek and decided to sit under the brush arbor that night.

Potter went to the preaching with some of his cowboy friends. They intended to wait until the preacher got the spirit moving and cause an uproar. Sure enough about halfway through the service, the cowboys began to heckle the preacher. Instead of joining them, Potter rose from his place and edged forward. His tall, demanding figure caused the crowd to listen as he said, "You better quieten down or you'll answer to me."

Potter said a strange feeling came over him right then, and he was converted that night. He turned an about-face to follow the Christian life from then on. Immediately he left his old way of behaving and began preaching in brush arbor meetings. Andrew had little formal education, so being a speaker or studying the Bible was an uphill challenge for him. The man who had raced horses as a kid, chased cattle as a teenager and driven a freight wagon as a man suddenly found himself studying long hours at night with the help of a coal oil lamp.

Jackson located the old preacher John who had first touched his soul while expounding the scriptures near York's Creek. When asked for help, this dear saint taught the rough cowboy how to prepare a sermon.

As early as 1859, the new Parson Potter preached at the town of Rio Frio, which was situated in Real County. Potter eventually moved to Lockhart, bought a farm, and was licensed to preach.

While he farmed, worked cattle, and preached, his neighbors had only one way to market cattle. They trailed them to northern markets. After being away from his childhood home in Missouri for a long time, he decided to make the trip. He rode the cattle trail toward Kansas in 1861. With a Bible in his saddlebags, Jackson hired on with a trail boss named Miller who paid him for 47 days on the trail. When the cattle were about 100 miles from his boyhood home, Potter left the herd.

Jackson's only family member home to greet him was his sister. Other friends who visited with him were amazed at the change they saw in this once rough gambler. Potter preached in his hometown and started a magical three-month revival where many souls were saved. His old neighbors saw a man before them who was like the apostle Paul, a biblical character who also made a drastic change in his life.

But Potter's trail drives had to stop temporarily because they were interrupted by the start of the Civil War. He served as a chaplain in the 32nd Texas Calvary of the Confederate Army. As a private in Capt. Stokely M. Homes's company of Col. Peter C. Wood's Texas Cavalry, Potter took part in battles of the Red River Campaign of 1864. Another group he served with was Col. Xavier B. DeBray's 27th Texas Cavalry.

Many a time Potter admonished the troops before a battle to ask the Lord for forgiveness and turn from their sins. Then his thoughts would turn to the harm that might befall some soldiers, and he prayed for the troopers that their lives might be spared in the upcoming battle. Potter said, "Boys, some of you may fall in this battle; in a few minutes you may be called to meet your Maker. Repent now and give your heart to Christ." He would continue by saying, "He is waiting to receive you. Oh, men, it's a solemn moment! You are facing death and eternity!" But when the commander of the troops sounded the call to attack, Potter put down his Bible, grabbed his gun and fought side by side with the soldiers.

When each battle was over, the parson's day really started. He prayed with the dying, urged the wounded to take heart and wrote letters for the bedridden men. He scarcely stopped to close his eyes or grab a plate of beans.

Once Potter's troops were camped near Brownsville, which had its own newspaper. Usually the troops expected the local printers to publish encouraging words about how hard the soldiers were fighting for their country. Instead, this local newspaperman criticized the soldiers in Potter's regiment. He was so mad at the accusations that he walked to the newspaper office, whipped the editor and planned to throw the printing press in the river. Just in the nick of time, some of the soldiers, including General Bee, stopped Potter before he carried out his intentions.

Potter's next battle was in the Red River campaign of 1864. In this skirmish, the soldiers experienced hunger and sickness. Some comrades died. As the parson suffered with the troops, he lived on bread, sugar and what berries he could find.

When the war was over, Jackson Potter returned to his home in Texas to preach again. He joined the Methodist West Texas Conference in 1866, and his first circuit was the Prairie Lea Circuit. As a circuit rider, Potter traveled many miles carrying only Bible, hymnbook, a few clothes, a pistol under his topcoat, and a rifle. He faced wild animals, the weather, and the Indians without an accident except a broken leg due to being unceremoniously thrown by an outlaw horse.

Potter recuperated from the fall and rode his horse, usually without a spill, to preach at various churches on the Prairie Lea Circuit. This little trip included Kerrville, Bandera, Mason, Brady, Boerne, and Uvalde.

The Methodist brethren had yearly conference meetings where lonely preachers like Potter had a chance to pat the other circuit riders on the back and listen to their tales of Indians on the trail and enduring cold camps between communities.

By 1872, Jackson Potter was known far and wide as a man who could get the job done with his gun or his Bible. The United States Congress grappled with the problem of frontier protection. A Texas congressman said to the lawmakers one time when they were in session, "Remove your regulars from the garrison on the Texas border; commission Jack Potter, a reclaimed desperado and now a Methodist preacher and Indian fighter; instruct him to choose and organize one hundred men; and Indian depredations along the Texas border will cease." Needless to say, Potter did not get his army to stand off the warriors.

Ranchers needed Jackson's help because the government seemed to help the Indians more than the cowman. The ranchers in the southwestern part of the Lone Star State were having a terrible time with Indians stealing their livestock. One group of cowboys, driving a herd of horses to the ranch headquarters west of San Angelo, heard the war cry of Indians. The horses broke away from their handlers, and the Indians followed the ponies. Once the cowboys realized what had happened, they opened fire on the thieves and killed two warriors.

The cowboys watched the Indians quickly disappear over a nearby hill. The warriors rode away while dropping some items they had recently received from Indian agents. In 1872 it was hard to explain to a rancher that the very same Indians who stole his livestock might also receive free rations from the United States government.

While Potter preached in Brady, he did not always expound the scriptures to saintly members in the church pew. Instead, he went where the "sinner" was most likely to be. The minutes of the Methodist Church Conference recorded that A. J. Potter visited Brady's Star Saloon at least once. After passing the day with the inhabitants, "Mr. Potter took off his guns, one on each side, laid them on a nearby chair and preached to the 'inmates' of the saloon."

In 1876 Potter preached fervently to a group in a camp meeting on Pipe's Creek in Bandera County. He usually preached alone, so he was surprised to see Rev. John Wesley DeVilbus rein his horse toward the gathering. After the service, Potter convinced DeVilbus to help him. The two preachers held forth in the pulpit for a number of days as they exhorted sinners to repent and turn to God.

These two ministers, very different in personality, cared deeply for each other. Potter was the take-charge, rough-and-rowdy man, whereas DeVilbus was quiet in spirit. DeVilbus, patient and caring, often smiled even when he was shedding tears and talking about the heavenly rest Christians would one day receive. During one service, DeVilbus listened to Potter's message and said, "God Bless you Bro. Potter. Your sermon did my soul good."

Potter complimented his friend as he said, "DeVilbus hated strife and contention and would never take part in the disputes of individuals or Christians."

This quiet man took a different road into the Texas ministry than Potter did. John Wesley DeVilbus, born in Maryland in 1818, learned the saddle-making trade at the age of thirteen. As his family moved southwestward, he was converted in a camp meeting in 1833. He studied awhile in a Methodist College in Augusta, Kentucky, and migrated to Texas in 1842. Within two years, he had a growing circuit around San Antonio. He married Talitha Ann Menefee in 1845, but her untimely death left him lonely. Two years later he married Martha Lucinda Kerr.

In the following years, he ministered to a variety of people. DeVilbus served at the Caldwell Colored Mission from 1852 to 1853 and preached at a German District the next several years. He truly loved all of God's children. DeVilbus spent at least twelve years on various circuits and later served as a college professor at Aranama College and as agent of Southwestern University.

Other preachers shared the same circuits as Potter did. Rev. J. H. Tucker was in the same neck of the woods as Potter because he was listed in church records as the preacher who received Susan Ogden as a member of the Brady Methodist Church by certificate on March 4, 1877. Undoubtedly several circuit riders crossed trails as they rode their horses to various churches. In fact, the Brady and Mason Missions were turned over to Tucker at the Corpus Christi Conference in the fall of 1877. At that meeting, presiding elder Bishop Wightmas created a new Methodist district that sent circuit riders from the Rio Grande River to the Colorado River. The preachers' horses had better be ready to cover a lot of miles as they rode toward their churches.

As circuits changed that particular fall, Potter moved to the Uvalde District, and Tucker took some of Jackson Potter's former circuits. Probably winter weather slowed the preaching because it was not until March 1878, that Potter met Tucker in Brady City and officially turned these two charges over to him. An elder of the church, W. T. Thornberry, wanted to visit the various circuits in Texas, but the Indians and marauding bandits had him a little shaky. He wanted another body in the buggy, or maybe another gun available, so he asked Potter to ride with him as the church records stated, "to protect him from Indians and desperadoes."

On this trip in March of 1878, the two men met at Center Point, traveled to Junction City in Kimble County and on to Brady City where they held a quarterly meeting there. Their trip continued through Mason and Fredericksburg and back to Center Point. No mention is made in the church minutes of any attacks on the two men.

Potter left the Elder and started on his own circuit. At this time, Potter worked alone as he traveled this large district that Bishop Wightmas created for him. The parson's route near Uvalde carried him through sparsely populated areas along the Rio Grande. Indians were often traveling the same trails as Potter.

On one particular trip, he had Bibles and provisions in a wagon pulled by two Spanish mules as he traveled through the rugged hills along his circuit. The wagon trail was in the bottom of the canyon with high hills on either side of the road that paralleled the preacher's progress. Four Indians spotted Potter from their position high up on one of those rocky points. They opened fire on him as he urged the mules along the trail below them.

Suddenly bullets flew around his mules and kicked dust up from the road. The parson jumped off the wagon and ran for cover. He scanned the rocks above him and carefully slipped up the hill until he could get the Indians in the sights of his gun. Potter shot one, hid himself in a thicket and finally wounded a second Indian. The other two warriors ran away. The parson was able to make the rest of the trip without any more interruptions.

The church bishops did not view fighting with Indians the same way Potter did. On one occasion, Potter was explaining how he confronted a band of Indians and dispersed them with the help of his Winchester. A bishop admonished him that scripturally speaking, "Our weapons are not carnal."

Potter replied quickly, "There were no Indians there when that was written."

Jackson Potter probably got a chuckle out of stories told about his preacher friend, J. H. Tucker, who took his place in the Mason and Brady Missions. Just as Potter sowed his wild oats riding racehorses, fighting in the Mexican War and freighting supplies across Texas before his conversion, Tucker had his rough side also.

J. H. Tucker, a native of Mississippi, came to Texas in time to drive a stage from San Antonio to El Paso in the 1850s. Somewhere between jobs he received the credentials to be called a medical doctor, and he tended the sick in the San Antonio–Uvalde area. Before 1859, the time of his accepting Christ as his Savior, Tucker was known for his irreligious life and daring. But the Lord called some interesting characters into his ministry.

When Tucker began to preach at the Brady City Mission, he increased the church roll from 24 to 101 in a one-year span. At times he preached to as many as 600 people in one congregation.

Tucker was as effective in the ministry as his friend, A. J. Potter. During his years as a circuit rider, Potter preached in many places. He was known to extol the virtues of his Lord in homes, churches, camp meetings, saloons and even fort chapels.

Circuit riders often looked for friendly ranch houses where they might stop as they rode from one community to another. Jackson Potter stopped to eat a meal with a family along his route if he found a willing cook. One day the parson was invited to stay for a meal by a family with children. When he offered the blessing before the meal and bowed his head, the little ones were surprised because they had not heard a prayer at mealtime. A little boy said to Potter, "Are you the preacher that talks to the plate?"

In 1880, Potter preached at San Angelo across the river from Fort Concho. At that time, San Angelo was a tiny village made up of saloons and gambling places that stayed open all day and night. It was a "raunchy" place. But Potter's family moved to San Angelo in 1883 although the community was still very rough.

Potter's first sermon in a saloon in San Angelo was well documented as the local yokels expected to give him a hard time. The parson

Reverend Andrew Jackson Potter preaching in a vacant saloon in San Angelo. Courtesy of the West Texas Collection at Angelo State University, San Angelo, Texas.

got permission to use an empty saloon for a service, so he fashioned seats out of two-by-twelve planks supported by empty beer kegs, got some kerosene lamps, and made a pulpit out of a big box. At the appointed time, the men began to congregate to see how the hecklers were going to take care of the parson.

Potter, a tall, gangling man with rugged features, walked into the building carrying his Winchester. He parked it nearby and pulled his forty-five "pet maker" out from under his tall black coat and laid it on his Bible. He told the congregation that "according to rumor, some un-regenerative sinners have bragged around town that they were going to break up this meeting. Maybe they will, but I'll guarantee one thing: they will be a bunch of mighty sick roosters before they get it done." Nobody bothered the preacher the rest of the evening.

The parson's own son, T. W. Potter, said of his father, "Daddy was called 'the fighting parson' because he stayed when other preachers had been scared away."

He stayed quite a while in this town by Fort Concho, too. After preaching in brush arbors and homes, Potter decided that San Angelo needed a Methodist church. The only trouble the plan had was the lack of money. The faithful believers could not come up with enough funds, so Potter decided to visit a saloon once more, the Blue Goose, to be exact. He entered the watering hole when it was busy, pounded his gun butt on the counter, and told them that each sinner there was going to help build a church. As he passed his hat, he carried his revolver. Nobody failed to kick in. One of the impresarios of the place was so impressed that he found another way for Potter to collect money. He led the parson up to a second-story room where the gambling had reached a serious level. Potter's helper roared to the men, "Boys, this here is Parson Potter, and he is going to build a church house. You know this town needs a church, so everyone is going to stop right now until everyone of you blankety blanks kicks in." He received quite a stack of money that time and the church was built.

Potter built churches better than he took care of his children. Through the years of marriage with Emily, A. J. Potter and his wife had fourteen children. Their dad was seldom home, so the burden of parenting fell solidly on Emily.

What time Potter was not in San Angelo, he visited other forts. He stayed a year at Fort Clark, a wild region of country between the Nueces River and the Rio Grande. This area harbored many outlaws and unsavory characters. Far from civilization, the people living there had to be pretty tough to stand the bandits and misfits who enjoyed this stretch of no-man's land. Although Texas finally claimed this area called the Nueces Strip, lawlessness still thrived while Potter roamed the area. The parson admitted that he did not have very good results while working there. He said, "I went to Fort Clark to preach several years ago and started without a member, and at the end of twelve months, I quit without a member."

Late one evening Potter rode into a town with a fort similar to Fort Concho or Fort Clark. At this place, the troops had received their pay

Reverend Andrew Jackson Potter raised funds to build the First Methodist Church of San Angelo, Texas, even though he resorted to visiting saloons to procure the necessary money. Courtesy of the First Methodist Church of San Angelo Texas Archives.

and were in good spirits. Potter saw soldiers, gamblers and crooks as he guided his horse down the dimly lit street. Most of the men knew him and said, "Here comes the fighting parson," or "Hold up, there, old pardner! Can't you give us a gospel song an' dance tonight?"

He answered that he would speak if they cleared him a space in some building. Of course they found a saloon and fixed seats of kegs and barrels. A drunk man felt obliged to help the preacher, so he shouted to the men nearby to come hear Potter so they could mend their ways. When his sermon was over, the characters wanted to "set him up" with a beer, but he declined. As a final gesture, they passed a cigar box to collect coins for his ministry.

Around 1883, Potter not only preached but also kept his hand in the ranching business. Now he had a son Jack who could help him on the trail drives. Jack and his dad were credited with establishing the Potter-Blocker Trail, a branch of the Western Trail. In his book, *Cattle Trails of the Old West,* Jack Potter said this trail was called the Potter-Bacon Cutoff.

Alfred Bacon was boss of the New England Livestock Company and decided to buy some Mexican cattle. These 3,000 head were to be delivered to Cheyenne, Wyoming. He hired Potter to drive them from Hebbronville, Texas, to their destination hundreds of miles northwest.

The trail that this group of cattle made was interesting. When the steers reached the Western Trail near present-day Alice, they passed through the only nearby town called Collins Station. They meandered across Texas so that they reached Albany, above Abilene, Texas, by June. At this point, Alfred Bacon sent word to Potter to change his course to save some time.

This part of the path, later called Potter-Blocker Trail, was shorter but did not have as many water holes as it crossed some desolate country. Bacon was determined to save about twenty days as he directed them to head northwest, past Rice Springs, cross the Brazos and on to Matador. From here, the cattle headed north to Field's Crossing on the Red River. At this point Potter had the cattle on Charles Goodnight's JA Ranch.

This area of the country had the name of "Winchester Quarantine" because many cattle coming from South Texas and Mexico carried the Texas Fever, which the Panhandle Ranches wanted no part of. Potter's cattle were suspected of having the fever, or at least being exposed to it, so Goodnight's manager turned the herd north to Amarillo, through the OX Ranch, and on to Tascosa. Potter and his herd passed Channing and Middle Water as they rode a course northwest until they changed directions and headed north to Perico Springs. The cattle left Texas south of Kenton, Oklahoma, passed through the corner of that state, visited Las Animas, Colorado, and made it to Cheyenne.

Since Potter's cattle finished the drive safely in 1883, two years later, Abner P. Blocker used a similar path to the northwest. Blocker passed through the large XIT range, and later the XIT Ranch used the same trail to move livestock to Montana where the XIT cattle pastured. This trail was used until the late 1880's. Homesteaders spoke out against the herds charging across their places, and railroads came to the Panhandle region at that time. By 1889, trail drives disappeared because the trains could take the cattle to their destination much quicker.

Reverend Potter stayed in the Concho River country and preached in many of the area religious gatherings, including the one at Sherwood, about 25 miles west of San Angelo. In newspaper columns of the *San Angelo Standard Times*, Potter was mentioned as the preacher at Sherwood's fifth Sunday meeting in June 1884. He returned in August to grace the pulpit at the local school, and he was later mentioned as the preacher in the same town the following December and January.

Potter continued to be active and preach in many area churches. On October 21, 1895, he preached in a tiny country church in Caldwell County called Tilman Chapel. His topic was "What think ye of Christ?" Before finishing the sermon, Potter said, "I think I have heard my last sermon: I am going home, I believe." As he said this, he fell leaving the pulpit, and his soul went home to be with God. He was buried in Walnut Creek Cemetery near Lockhart.

While Potter spent many days in the saddle riding the rough canyons around Uvalde, another Methodist circuit rider followed his trails. The 1880 U. S. Census listed Francis Marion York as twenty-six years old and single.

Parson York did not stay single very long. Wedding bells rang when soon he married his girl friend. He and his missus eventually became proud parents of two daughters. York lived wherever a vacant house appeared. Sometimes that meant setting up housekeeping in an empty ranch house some distance from his church. The parson was not always blessed with enough money to feed both his family and a horse.

For this reason, York walked a lot of miles to his preaching engagements. His family remembers him getting up early on Sunday morning, so he could get to church on time. The distance he walked was much too long for his wife to tag along and carry the children. His family said he always left the house on Sunday morning looking starched and pressed, just the way a preacher ought to look.

By the day's end, York came home looking like a different man. His clothes were wilted, and he walked bare-foot while carrying his shoes thrown over his shoulder with laces tied together.

York must have had a financial windfall later in life because he is remembered as proudly driving a car as an older man. York thought a lot of fenders and other accessories belonging to his vehicle were excess baggage, so he removed them.

He never quite mastered how to back out gently from a parking lot. His granddaughter, Bertie Langford, said he roared out driving backward with so little regard for the other drivers around him that he barely missed having a wreck several times. His driving techniques were so bad that a policeman had to reprimand him. When approached by the lawman, York turned to him and said, "Oh, I'm just a crazy old fool."

What he lacked in driving skills, he more than made up for in other areas. York was well loved by his congregation, and he knew his Bible well. This man of English descent poured over the verses in Proverbs as well as other beloved books. He memorized much of the Bible. To this day, family members lovingly preserve his Bible. Bertie Langford said, "It is worn and many pages are stained with dark smudges where he handled it."

Even though York worked hard and knew the scriptures, life was not easy for his household. His first wife died and was buried at Leakey. Francis York married again, this time to Sarah Conn. She was a strict disciplinarian, just the type of person that most churches felt preachers' wives should be like. The Yorks had two more daughters to make a family of four girls.

York moved about as he preached in Rocksprings and finally in San Angelo. He may have had a home for a while near Santa Anna as he also outlived his second wife. When she died, York buried her in Santa Anna.

Whether God sent Potter riding through the countryside or York walking down a dusty trail, He had great spokesmen that carried his gospel to Texas. Men from Europe also felt the desire in their hearts to preach God's word in this great state. When they landed on Texas soil, life had some interesting turns and twists for them.

4

EUROPEAN IMMIGRANT PREACHERS: 1850–1900s

People who left Europe for the new land called Texas made the journey with a big helping of hope packed in their suitcases. Such immigrants hoped for more food for their family, more land to cultivate, and most of all, a place they could worship God as they saw fit.

But Germans coming to Texas from their homeland or nearby Austria met challenges they did not expect. They found diverse religions in this new land as circuit-riding preachers knocked on their doors almost as soon as they landed. By 1840 many Germans had embraced the Methodist theology, probably because this group of preachers pounded on their doors more than others did. In no time at all, the German Methodists became a part of the Methodist Churches in Texas. This group had their own German district, which included eleven churches by 1855.

As early as 1854, some German immigrants complained that they wanted to hear a Lutheran sermon like the ones they heard in the old country. These unhappy churchgoers were ecstatic when Rev. Johann G. Ebinger visited their community and preached to them Lutheran theology. For a few minutes, Ebinger took them back to the cathedrals ringing with song and scripture they knew so well in their homeland. Ebinger preached at a community called "Berlin." Germans affectionately used the names of their favorite cities in their old homeland to identify their new towns in America.

Not to be overshadowed, the Baptists also infiltrated the immigrants and tried to influence their worship with another European named J. Frank Kiefer. He emigrated from Milheim, Prussia, where he was born August 13, 1833, into a Catholic family. In 1850 he followed an older brother to Texas. Keifer made an abrupt change in his religious life after coming to this new land. At the town of Independence, Kiefer worshipped at a Baptist Church. He embraced their beliefs and was baptized June 6, 1854. Soon thereafter he was licensed in Texas to preach by an Independent Baptist Church.

Feeling a need for instruction, Kiefer entered Baylor University in his hometown of Independence in 1857. His ability to speak the German language impressed the school's administration. They realized that this twenty-four-year-old man knew the German language better than most of them in the school. Kiefer was asked to teach German, which he did. Although he taught, preached and took classes, Kiefer stopped short of getting his degree. He met a pretty lady named Amanda M. Allen from Huntsville, and they married April 19, 1858. Their home was blessed with thirteen children.

The Baptist State Convention of Texas sent Kiefer, now labeled a missionary, to German Texans in 1858–1859. Since this preacher adapted to ways of the new land, he held religious services for these citizens as a circuit rider. At Greenvine, five miles southeast of Burton in Washington County, Kiefer conducted a revival in 1860. His effort to bring people to the Lord must have succeeded because the first German Baptist Church in Texas originated in that community the following year.

Many people he visited had no medical care, so Kiefer decided he could help solve that problem with some hours of study. He burned "the midnight oil" as he pored over his books learning anatomy and the alchemy of medicines at Galveston Medical School. Finally, Dr. Kiefer graduated March 1867, and "hung his shingle" so the town knew he was a licensed medical doctor. In Harris County, Dr. Kiefer practiced medicine during the week and preached on Sundays for one year.

The next several years Kiefer was very busy as a missionary and church builder. He ministered particularly to special groups such as Indian, German and Mexican. On his circuit, the language could change drastically from one church to another. He and Frank J. Gleiss started a church in Washington County called Cedar Hill Baptist.

Kiefer was too busy with his preaching to continue as a medical doctor, so he eventually dropped his practice. Although he no longer visited the sick, various medicines continued to interest him. While preaching in Texas, he experimented with chemicals and created different medicines in his alchemy shop. In 1880 he invented a purgative called the Kiefer Pill. Its use was so successful that he produced it in a factory in Independence, Texas.

After preaching to Germans in Texas for many years, Kiefer felt the need to hold revivals in Europe. From money made from his pills and other donations, he planned four winter trips to Germany and Russia where he preached revivals. Before attempting these long trips, he sold his farm. Kiefer accomplished so much as a preacher and humanitarian that Waco University granted him an honorary doctorate of divinity in 1884. In the next few years, Kiefer slowed his preaching schedule. He eventually moved to Roby, Texas, in 1889, where he intended to retire. His wife Amanda passed away in 1899.

However, Kiefer put himself in idling gear for only a short time. A year and a half later, he married Mrs. Eugene Evans and became active in the community. He was known as a preacher, doctor and county health officer of Fisher County by 1902. This workhorse did not slow down again until he passed away November 25, 1909, and was buried in the Roby Cemetery.

Kiefer blazed the trails for other European preachers who came to this big state filled with endless prairies and people who did not know God. Up to this point, most immigrants coming into Texas came as one or two families traveling in wagons or as one man astride a horse. But that situation was about to change.

In 1854, Johann Kilian brought his family, as well as 550 Wendish-German immigrants with him, to Texas from his church congregation in Upper Lusatia. This European area belonged to Saxony in the south and Prussia in the north. In order to escape religious persecution, these people called Wends, settled in Lee County and eventually called their new town Serbin, meaning "Wendish land."

Their leader, Johann Kilian, entered the ministry in Prussia in the 1830s, a time when members of his religion, Old Lutheran, felt oppressed by the government for their beliefs. Most people in that area of Prussia were coerced to merge with various Protestant churches.

Kilian said, "No" to this pressure to conform, so he left Lusatia. He spoke both Wend and German and was quite educated for his day, so he made a good leader. Kilian graduated from the Gymnasium of Bautzen and received his theology training from the University of Leipzig. He began to preach in his homeland in 1837. By 1840, the government lifted its oppression against Old Lutherans to some extent. Now church members could worship together as a congregation, but each group was rather small. The government issued some aggravating restrictions on these churches: among other rules, they could not have a bell to ring or a steeple on their churches. By 1848, Kilian was pastor of two churches in Prussia. He also rode a circuit to visit congregations in several other towns. While still in his homeland, Kilian published a number of religious works.

Over a period of years, he felt the restrictions of the government limited his congregation too much, so he left his printing press in the old country to travel westward. The 550 original Wends sailed on a ship named *Ben Nevis*. When Kilian moved his group to Texas at present Lee County, he immediately affiliated himself with the Missouri Synod Lutheran Church. His congregation was considered the mother colony of Wends in Texas.

Reverend Johann Kilian founded the Wendish Community at Serbin, Texas. Courtesy of the Texas Wendish Heritage Museum Archives at Serbin, Texas.

At first their community on the Gotcher Trace was called Low Pin Oak Settlement. By 1885 the group needed more land, so Carl Lehman and John Dube purchased 4,000 acres on the Wendish people's behalf. Carl and John were in the real estate business, selling farms and town lots to the Wendish people. Now that the colony had space for their homes, they took care of other needs.

The Lutheran congregation bought 95 acres on which to build a church and a school. The impressively large Lutheran Church building watched many generations of Wend children pass through its doors. For thirty years Kilian pastored the Lutheran church in this location, which became known as Serbin when the post office was established in 1860.

Johann Killian preached in both Wendish as well as German dialect in this St. Paul Lutheran Church in Serbin. He knew the children needed an education, so Killian developed a parochial school in the same town as the church and taught there for twelve years. The Wendish people were in Texas, but they lived close together, went to church and school together and mostly married Wends.

These immigrants were good farmers who raised mainly corn and cotton as a cash crop. During the Civil War, they transported cotton all the way to Matamoras and Houston to sell on the market there. The successful farmers brought home needed goods as well as gold coins from their trip to the gulf coast.

In the following years, Serbin increased in size with two general stores, three blacksmiths, two wheelwrights, a meat market, a carpenter and a physician. A visitor to the streets of Serbin saw the same sites a person would see if he visited any other early-day Texas town. However, the spoken word was definitely Wendish or German. The impressive St. Paul Lutheran Church building was the first congregation of the Missouri Synod in Texas. Many Lutheran church leaders found their buggies heading toward Serbin because it was the site of many church meetings called synodical conventions.

In 1890 newly laid train tracks belonging to the San Antonio and Aransas Pass Railway bypassed Serbin and swung two miles east. Almost immediately stores and family dwellings started the slow migration to be nearer the tracks. One storeowner after another moved his business to the track. Large wooden poles, placed under the building in a parallel fashion, were used to move the structures. Teams of mules or oxen slowly pulled the building forward. As the building moved off the last log, it was placed in front of the building, and the structure continued to move forward. As more store buildings moved toward the shiny rails, a new town emerged, appropriately called New Serbin or Serbin Switch. When the new train station appeared, this young community was renamed Northup. With all the transformation of the town, one structure remained at the same location. Membership at the St. Paul Lutheran Church held steadfast. As late as 1990, it had 555 members and 78 students in its school.

Just as Johann Kilian rode the back roads of Prussia as a circuit rider, he also saddled his horse so he could visit several Wendish communities in Texas, particularly New Ulm and Bastrop. At that time, groups of the Wend people were scattered in the communities of Noack and Macedonia in Williamson County, at Twin Mountain in Coryell County and at the towns of Swiss Alp and Warda in Fayette County.

Before leaving Prussia, Johann Kilian married Maria Groeschel in 1848. They had four children while living in Prussia, but only one survived. In America four more children were born and survived infancy. By 1872, Kilian's son Gerhard took over some of the teaching duties at the Wendish school. Son Hermann became pastor in his father's place in 1884. A few months later, the apostle who led his people westward, Johann Kilian, could lead no more. He died on September 12, 1884.

Another immigrant to Texas in the 1850s who eventually became a preacher was Carl Urbankte. His life began December 3, 1831, in Bielitz, Austria. Born as the sixth of eleven children in a hardworking family of weavers, Urbankte was sitting in front of a loom at an early age. He also found out rather quickly what a long workday meant.

The industrial revolution of 1848, coupled with political unrest, caused him to question whether he wanted to remain in his homeland. Factories turned out cloth so much faster than his family could that Urbankte wondered how they would survive. Orders for their cloth declined. Another worry for him was the draft. He neared the age where he would be called into eight long years of customary but forced military duty in his home country.

He read articles about other Germans emigrating to Texas, a place of new opportunities, so he quietly planned his trip to this new land. After working hard to save his money, Urbankte gained ship passage to

America. However, the lengthy journey, scarcity of drinking water, and the tossing of the ship by storms made him wonder about his sanity. When he almost reached the conclusion that his journey was a mistake, he landed at Galveston. Knowing not a soul and speaking only German, Urbankte discovered real loneliness. Job-hunting frustrated him but he worked first building railroad embankments and then as a farmhand.

After months of isolation, he found the German settlement of Millheim and felt at home as he heard his native tongue spoken once more. From working on farms, Urbankte moved to jobs in a cotton gin, corn mill and sawmill with salaries from ten to twenty-five dollars a month.

Over a period of three years, he collected enough money to make a down payment on land near San Felipe. This little town had been crushed by the Mexican troops during the War for Independence and rebuilt to some extent by the time he saw it for the first time. Even though the Brazos River flowed nearby and brought some commerce to the area, Urbankte would not see the citizens of San Felipe using the courthouse. About ten years before he arrived, the county seat moved to Bellville.

He was not bothered by the decline of San Felipe because two more important projects competed for his attention. When visiting Carl Urbankte, a person would see him either on a ladder mending his farmhouse or plowing his farmland. In 1859 he was quite satisfied because he now had enough money to send for his father and brother.

With family and land, he should have been happy, but in his book, *Texas Is the Place for Me,* he admitted that his relationship with God was incomplete. To make matters worse, Urbankte received a letter from his sister saying that his sweetheart in Austria married an architect instead of waiting for him. His world fell apart even though he had a nice home and a successful farm.

Ignoring God's call for his life, the young immigrant spent much of his time pining over lost affections. As he dreamed about his true love's marriage to another, Urbankte woke up mad at the world one day and took his feelings out on a cow that needed penning so he could milk her. He hit her with a whip. The end of the leather weapon twirled around and hit her eye. Urbankte realized he had hurt an innocent creature and expected God to retaliate. Later that day while plowing, Urbankte felt the horn of his oxen hit his eye. It swelled so much that he could not see a thing. For two years, Urbankte suffered from pain and double vision due to the accident with the oxen. He decided that God was talking directly to him through this ordeal.

In 1862, a young preacher came to visit his community and spoke in church. Carl Urbankte, raised in the Lutheran Church, thought of worship as just a ritual. He never took it seriously. He had even made laughing remarks to friends that he did not believe in God. Although Urbankte told the visiting preacher about his atheist views, the young man of the cloth did not argue. He simply left a tract called "Is the Bible inspired by God?" for the doubting Urbankte to read.

When Urbankte opened this little book, he became totally consumed with its contents and read until 2 a.m. in the morning. In the solitude of his own home, the saving power of God spoke to him, and he was convicted of his sin.

He had a hunting buddy named August Scheurich. The two men would hunt and fish on Saturday after work. This friend lost three children within a period of ten days to diphtheria, so when Urbankte tried to tell his fishing friend about Christ, his words floated away. The man was bitter and blamed God for his loss of family members. Months later, Urbankte gave him the little book that had warmed his own soul, but the words had a different effect on August than they did on Carl Urbankte.

Words in a book did not convince Scheurich at that time, but ever so slowly he did warm up to the saving power of Christ, and eventually the two friends talked and walked with Jesus together.

Once Urbankte was a born-again believer, he wanted to go to church, but a trip to the nearest Lutheran church required a long journey. Many of the German-speaking Christians attended a nearby Methodist church, so Urbankte did also. On the day the preacher held services at the German church, most families carried boxes of food and dishes for their noonday meal and bundles of corn-top fodder for their horse.

Usually a bell rang for services to start. The congregation sang hymns, knelt in prayer while the minister talked to God, and listened to the twenty-third Psalm recited in German. After the preacher read his text aloud, the ushers carried Stetson hats down the aisle to receive the collection. The minister had their rapt attention during his sermon because they loved to hear the German language tell about God.

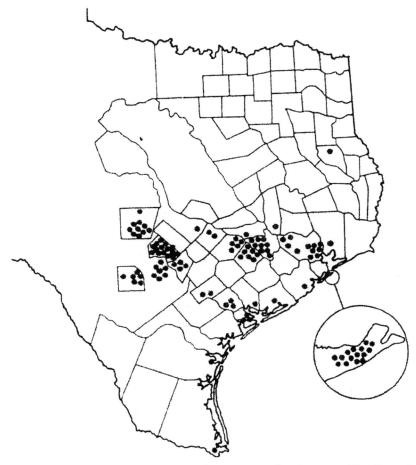

German Element in Texas as of 1850 (1 dot = 100 people). Courtesy of The General Libraries, The University of Texas at Austin.

Some nearby citizens advocated that these people should learn English and worship in English. However, as Dr. Gilbert J. Jordan from Fredericksburg explained, "It is one thing to learn to speak and understand a new language, but it is something else again to preach and pray in this acquired language." The immigrants refused to worship in English because the Lord continued to speak in German to the people, and they prayed to him in German also.

Something else happened to Urbankte in the early 1860s: he became involved in the Confederate Army. He and his brother Gustav had questions about slavery but chose to fight for the South. At one time, Urbankte actually wrote, "I could not remain in a church that sanctioned slavery, and sought to defend its position by the scriptures." He wrote this when he discovered that the Northern Methodist Church was anti-slavery. The Civil War was harsh to some people such as Urbankte's brother Gustav. When he fought for the Confederate Army, he was captured and imprisoned for two long years in the Northern states.

Even though Carl Urbankte returned from fighting and had his life right with the Lord, by 1865 he realized he needed something more. This thirty-four-year-old man wanted a wife. He owned a comfortable home and owed no debts on his farm, but his first love, a lady in the old country, was the only woman he ever loved.

Now Urbankte desired a mate to love and care for, so he prayed to God about the problem. In his mind, he believed that God would provide him a beautiful young bride. Urbankte's father doubted that God would send his son a wife just because he prayed for one, but Urbankte replied to the older man, "Why not? Is He not the same God who sent Rebecca to Isaac?"

However, he met a widow with three children. This woman was a humble Christian, but he did not love her and told her so. After talking to her, Urbankte admitted, "If you want to become my wife, trusting God, who can direct our affections and unite our hearts in love, say yes. But if you are afraid to marry me under these conditions, say no, and no one shall ever find out what has passed between us."

He was surprised when she revealed to him that she had been thinking about him before he ever proposed, and she believed God had his hand in their decision. They sealed their engagement with a handshake and a kiss. They were married amid relatives and friends August 15, 1865.

Urbankte's religion as a child in a Lutheran church in his homeland finally began to have meaning as a Methodist minister helped him understand the Bible. Soon this immigrant was asked to lead the Bible studies in his local church when the regular pastor could not attend.

A church asked him to preach. They actually wanted him to stand behind the pulpit and explain the word of God. He visited small churches near his home and got his feet wet as he administered the word of God to a hungry congregation. Urbankte had testimonial meetings at some churches and neighbors discussed how these speeches from the heart affected them. Pretty soon, members of other churches wanted to do the same.

At the time Urbankte received a preacher's license, he felt more confidence speaking before people. A larger church in Beeville asked him to fill the pulpit, and he said, "Yes," without hesitation. Beeville had a courthouse, a post office, a number of businesses and a Masonic Lodge. Carl Urbankte was no longer preaching in a tiny village.

A strange thing happened when Urbankte arrived for the service. He saw two preachers, as well as many knowledgeable church members, present in the pews. He gamely made his way to the podium and read his scripture aloud, but when he started to speak, he forgot all his well-rehearsed words. He had to ask the presiding elder, Rev. Grote, to finish the service. If Carl Urbankte could have dug a hole in the church's floor, he would have crawled right in.

Urbankte, very disappointed at his inability to speak, knew he would never preach again. However, the church at Beeville asked him to preach the following Sunday. Although he lacked confidence and thought a run to the door seemed like a good idea, Urbankte led in prayer and preached a sermon on Matthew 16: 15–18. He remembered most of his rehearsed words and preached much better this time than he had before.

When Urbankte and his wife had been married a year, they planned to celebrate. God had been calling him to leave his hometown and preach in new places, but his wife did not want them to move. Just before their anniversary, Emma, his wife's daughter became ill with scarlet fever and died. Within a few days, one of their sons complained of chills and fever. He took a turn for the worst and lay unconscious on his bed.

Urbankte felt that God had been calling him to preach elsewhere and his refusal had caused the sickness of the children. His wife realized what was happening and said, "Never again will I utter a word against anything the Lord wants you to do. I deeply regret my folly and have asked God's forgiveness. We wanted to stay on the farm for the sake of our children, and now God shows us that He can take away that which we put up as an excuse not to do his will."

Their son recovered and within a few days, Urbankte was asked to become a circuit rider. He began his preaching career with new enthusiasm just as changes took place in the Methodist church over the slavery issue. The Northern Methodists were against it, and the South was for it. By 1866, some churches withdrew from the Southern Methodist congregations and returned to the original Methodist Episcopal Church. This action caused the small German Methodist churches to be poverty stricken and forced to build new buildings because the Methodist South confiscated their church houses.

Carl Urbankte met with about ninety other preachers at Houston on January 3, 1867, for the Texas Mission Conference. As heads bowed to pray to God, he was in the presence of black, white, and brown fellow worshippers. Former slaves made up part of the group that day. At this conference, Urbankte's assignment became the Roundtop area where he was to visit and establish as many new congregations as possible. This area was 30 miles westward from his home, but as a circuit rider, he did not argue with God anymore.

The first year, he preached in any farmhouse whose family would give him the opportunity. His new friends invited people in the neighborhood to hear his sermons At times, he had no horse or wagon and had to walk as far as twenty-two miles over an ice-covered road. He felt a calling to live near a new congregation at Rabbs Creek, but there was no house suitable for him, the preacher.

Finally, Carl Urbankte found a vacant hut where the wind blew through the cracks, the roof was leaky, and a calf had previously used it as a barn. With much fear of rejecting God's calling, he moved his wife, two older children and a new baby into their humble quarters. They chinked mud in the cracks, cleaned the cabin, and converted another small adjoining building into a kitchen so that the buildings began to look like a home. Urbankte preached in a vacant Lutheran Church in Bastrop and in another German community nine miles from town.

His wife became very ill, so he pulled double duty. He cooked for the family as well as circulating around to his various congregations. He preferred to cook outside as he did when he was a single man, but even so he fixed enough food to last his family for several days. He stayed near his wife's bed one night late into the wee hours of morning because she was very ill.

However, at four in the morning she urged him to go make his rounds preaching. Urbankte preached at Bastrop, eighteen miles from home, at ten in the morning, at three he preached at Piney, and he made his way home by ten that night. He had preached twice and rode forty miles. He and his horse were both exhausted.

Finding a building in which to hold services in some communities was very hard. In Brenham, Urbankte had people tell him they wanted to have church services, but they had no building. In this community, he felt comfortable because many German immigrants called this town home. He inquired about vacant buildings, an oddity because many had been burned during Reconstruction days. Finally a man offered his vacant joiner's shop. When Urbankte looked inside the building, he found a dirty place with boards lying around and windows he could not see through.

He got help to clean the building and make seats out of boards. Soon Urbankte had a congregation of fifty or more people to hear him preach. Eventually, the summer days rolled around and the building was too hot, so a new church building was added to the prayer list. He heard about a banker that might help them financially, but when he found out the congregation was not Southern Methodist, he would not give them any money. Urbankte scrounged around for dollars to aid his building fund and finally received enough help to keep the workers paid and get the church built.

Carl Urbankte spent nine years traveling about Texas to check on the churches while he carried the title, "presiding elder." He would start on a trip riding a train, but many journeys included a ride on a stagecoach, a wagon and a horse before he finished his journey. He visited the storm-torn Indianola in 1875 when the town and a new Methodist church were blown apart by a hurricane.

As he traveled in Central and West Texas, he saw the cowboys who rode for days without seeing another human. Urbankte experienced Indian raids, and bandits of various sorts. Two railroad accidents made him very hesitant to ride the iron horse. In later years, he felt very nervous when any train started to sway and jerk. When these days drew to a close, he helped organize Blinn College to teach young men to be preachers. This Austrian preacher lived to the age of eighty-one before he was called home to the Lord.

Although Carl Urbankte was able to make the adjustment from living in the old country to life in the new one, others could not. Some German immigrants had a hard time in America and clung to old allegiances even when World War I started. Holding tight to beliefs taught in their mother country, as well as naming communities after the ones they left behind in the Old Country, eventually got the Germans in some trouble in America. German immigrants established a community on the eastern side of Stonewall County. They tilled soil that had never seen a plow and named their new home Brandenburg after one of their cherished towns in the Old Country. As the railroad's appearance moved the town's location two miles west to the Northwestern Railway Company's tracks, the community increased in size. Brandenburg flourished as it added a gin, post office and school.

Then World War I embroiled the country in anti-German sentiment. Feelings against anything pertaining to this nationality ran very high. Non-Germans accused the people of the Brandenburg settlement of not being loyal to the United States. Some of their neighbors thought the German immigrants were partial to their home country, even to the point of sending information back to Europe secretly. A few German families were accused of being spies. Sentiment against the immigrants got so strong that the town finally changed its name from Brandenburg to Old Glory. Such a patriotic name silenced the critics.

German preachers, as well as German citizens, persevered in Texas in spite of anti-German sentiments. Another group of people who felt some hatred aimed at them as they migrated to Texas were the black ministers.

5

NEGRO IMMIGRANT
PREACHERS: 1850–1900s

Most Southern Negro preachers rode their horses westward to escape slavery. While black ministers from the North had the same destination, they were hoping that life might have more opportunities in this rustic state of Texas than in the homes they left behind. However, black preachers ran into problems in Texas. Some black men of the cloth felt hatred aimed toward them almost as soon as they stepped across the state line. These preachers soon found out that some Texans had a different way of looking at things.

Some black ministers like Benjamin Franklin Williams came to Texas as a slave. Although he was born in the Deep South, Brunswick County, Virginia, in 1819, his owners took Williams with a wagonload of other slaves on a long journey. He passed through South Carolina, then Tennessee and eventually made his way to Colorado County, Texas, in 1859. He dusted off the trail dirt and found himself at a new home west of Houston. The work his owner forced on him was no different from what he experienced in Virginia; long hours in the field felt the same to his aching back.

When freedom finally came, Benjamin Williams looked around at the possibilities of a new life. Although he could have hit the road to see distant lands, a young woman changed his mind. Williams's eyes fell on a certain Caroline. Not too many months of courting took place until he married Caroline Williams in Colorado County. These newlyweds shared the same last name long before the matrimonial vows were spoken. He took the worship experience seriously when he attended the nearby black church on Sunday. Soon after emancipation took place, Williams knew what he wanted to do as his first act as a free man. He told his church friends that he wanted to be a circuit-riding Methodist preacher.

Soon Williams not only had a wife, but he also had new work. He felt successful in his new calling because the Wesley Methodist Chapel in Austin asked him to be their preacher when its doors opened in 1865. But membership in this church had stringent requirements: people could not join this church unless they were Republicans.

Williams decided he would combine religion and politics, if he had to. He spoke on behalf of his race and became very involved in the Loyal Union League. This organization took a stand on how its members voted. They were to vote for no one who supported the Confederacy, so they could side only with Union men for office.

Although Williams pushed the Union candidates, the election of 1866 did not go their way. The reason the outcome was against them was because, in part, blacks still could not vote. By 1868 Williams climbed the ladder of success as he held the position of vice president of the Loyal Union League. He informed the white Unionists as to how politics were doing in the black-belt area.

Benjamin Williams received more recognition among the Loyalists when he won a seat on the Constitutional Convention of 1868-1869. Reconstruction was the big issue for everybody and was on the minds of all people to whom Williams spoke. Benjamin Williams was very involved in the selection of new officers in local government, a fact that tried the patience of some white leaders.

This Negro preacher, Williams, was stubborn according to some white people. They tried to change his opinion about issues like licensing doctors and maintaining equality for all, but he held fast to his convictions. Benjamin Williams soon earned the title of one who never backed down from a cause.

Although Williams was a preacher, not a doctor, he felt that medical doctors needed more education than many received in the late 1800s. At his first opportunity, Williams stood before the Texas Legislature and introduced a resolution that would require doctors to be certified by a medical board. Many a practitioner of that time studied medical books and did the best he could to help the sick, but Williams felt the education of a medical doctor should be on a higher level.

As a part of the Executive Committee of the Constitutional Convention, the parson also proposed that the Constitution have a provision that banned racial segregation in all public places. He wanted this law to be enforced by the licensing powers of the state, counties and cities. Williams was the Martin Luther King of the 1800s as he used his pulpit to try to bring equality to all people.

However, his leadership was in vain because the majority of the delegates did not share his vision. Williams was so discouraged that he walked out of the Constitutional Convention before it was over and refused to sign the constitution. However, his ability to explain his ideas effectively made him a popular man.

When the time came to elect Texas legislators, voters looked toward Williams. In 1871 he was elected to the Twelfth Legislature and represented Lavaca and Colorado counties. He moved his church membership to another town and served as a legislator in the Sixteenth Legislature of 1879 from a different district. At that time, he represented Waller, Fort Bend and Wharton counties. Williams's last jaunt in the legislature was in 1885 when he represented Waller and Fort Bend counties. During his tenure, he tried to push legislation that would help both agricultural and skilled laborers. Williams had church circuits as well as political ones, so his horses and buggy kept the road hot.

After the 1885 session, Williams stepped down from the role of congressman, but he continued to preach and speak as an evangelist. His last endeavor was that of land speculation. He and his friends helped to settle and develop the town of Kendleton.

This little burg, once the site of a plantation owned by William E. Kendal, was situated in Fort Bend County, fourteen miles southwest of Rosenburg. In 1860 Kendal divided his holdings into several small farms, which he sold to former slaves. This predominantly black community received a boost when the New York, Texas and Mexican Railway passed through Kendleton. The town soon had several buildings, including a post office.

As if he were not busy enough, Williams wanted one more job. He became postmaster of Kendleton in 1884. As time passed, the parson would see several general stores, as well as a Methodist and a Baptist church erected in the town he helped build. In 1903 the school population listed two schools for twelve white students and three schools for 202 black students. Williams succeeded in land development as well as preaching.

As more black men took their place behind the pulpit, one particular religion became very popular among the Negroes. The African Methodist Episcopal Church, which was the oldest African-American Christian group in the United States, had an interesting history. Long before the Civil War, thoughts came together in the minds of Negroes in the United States that they needed their own denomination.

During those slavery times, black people often tried to worship with white people only to suffer discrimination and physical abuse. If they were allowed in the church at all, black people were told to occupy the last pews in the church. Richard Allen led this movement in 1878, when he and other blacks left the Methodist Episcopal Church to found the Free African Society.

Richard Allen was happy to lead this group, but surprising to him, others in the church pulled away from his theology. As the churches splintered, two separate church groups developed. Allen felt that this new organization of believers favored the teachings of Quakers more than Methodist Episcopal beliefs. This caused him eventually to lead six black congregations to establish the African Methodist Episcopal Church in 1799. This group designated Richard Allen as their first bishop.

Richard Allen was very opinionated and strong willed. Some churches, in the newly founded denomination and their members, disagreed with him and finally broke away from the African Methodist Episcopal Church. Even so, when Allen died, the A.M.E. Church numbered over 7,000 members in the United States. The church was so large and financially successful that they sent missionaries to Canada, the Caribbean and West Africa. This black church was able to send missionaries back to the very country where their ancestors once lived.

Into this scenario of new black churches came Monroe Franklin Jamison. Although born into slavery at his 1848 Georgia home, he eventually found his freedom as well as his preaching voice. Even as a young person, he never seemed to be bothered about speaking before a group. As a twenty-two-year-old preacher, Jamison used his fiery, jubilant delivery to draw people to God.

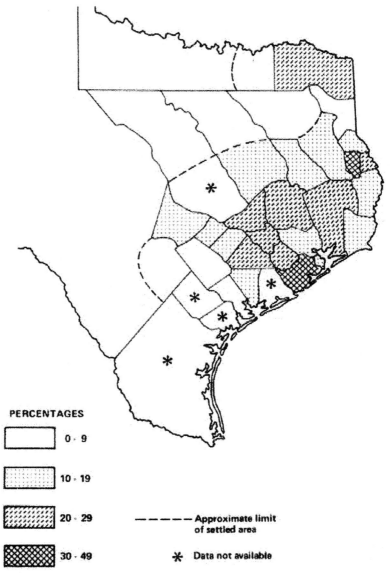

PERCENTAGES

☐ 0 - 9

▒ 10 - 19

▓ 20 - 29

▨ 30 - 49

— — — — Approximate limit
of settled area

✳ Data not available

Black Slaves as a Percentage of Total Population of Texas in 1840. Courtesy of The General Libraries, The University of Texas at Austin.

Somewhere between messages, young Jamison felt the wanderlust hit him hard. By 1872 he sensed the urge to travel westward so much that he saddled his horse and started down the dangerous trail westward. This lone figure, riding horseback, knew little about the many outlaws lurking along the trail, not to mention the possibility of renegade Indians who escaped the reservations.

However, after a long, weary journey, Jamison reined in his horse safely near Marshall, Texas, and decided this area of the East Texas piney woods would be his home. He met other black Methodist ministers busily building churches in the area also. Monroe Jamison was drawn to the African Methodist Episcopal Church.

Since the General Conference of the Methodist Episcopal Church decided in 1866 that black members could have their own congregations and conferences if they wanted to, church building began to take place in Texas with great gusto. The sound of hammers banging against lumber cut through the air far and wide. Finally black people could worship as they saw fit in buildings created by their own hands.

Jamison and his fellow pastors decided to form several Colored Methodists Episcopal circuits, which included the Black Jack Circuit, Hillard Circuit, Center Circuit and Antioch Circuit. Spreading God's word went well in the eastern areas of Texas, and Jamison's "Alabama style" of joyous preaching appealed to the poor people of those backwoods communities. Eventually, he was nicknamed "fighting Joe" because he loved to debate doctrine with other preachers.

By 1875 the East Texas Conference of Colored Methodist Episcopal Church was going strong under Bishop Isaac Lane. As a part of this group, Jamison watched over his flock at the Marshall and Longview Stations. When his job was more secure, he married Minerva A. Flinnoy January 14, 1874. The following year found the newlyweds in Dallas where Jamison built the first Colored Methodist Episcopal Church. In the 1876 annual conference in his own church, Jamison was named presiding elder.

This fiery minister spent less time now as a circuit rider and more as a student. In 1908 he was awarded the Doctor of Divinity degree from Texas College in Tyler. Now Jamison turned to writing as he edited the *Christian Index* for the Colored Methodist Episcopal Church and the *Christian Advocate* for the East Texas Conference. Jamison's full life drew to a close, and he died in 1918. Jamison was buried in the Pleasant Hill Cemetery.

Many black ministers during the Reconstruction years pushed for equality through their sermons, through the printing press and through politics. Rev. Jacob Fontaine was no exception, for he used all means he could muster to spread his message to black people.

When Fontaine was born in Arkansas in 1808, he was a slave. As bad as that life was, he benefited from knowing the families he served. His first owners were the Tuttle and Isaacs families, but eventually owner Rev. Edward Fontaine influenced young Jacob the most. This preacher was the great-grandson of Patrick Henry. He moved his household and slaves to Austin, Texas, in 1839.

Edward Fontaine had the prestigious job of personal secretary to Texas's President, Mirabeau B. Lamar. Due to Edward's position, his slave, Jacob Fontaine, had opportunities to listen as his master discussed political questions of the day.

Jacob and his wife Melvina had other opportunities to meet interesting people when they lived on the Woodlawn plantation. Their nearby neighbor was ex-governor Elisha M. Pease. Melvina was a housekeeper at the Pease's house and cooked at their mansion. While working at these jobs, the Fontaine family met influential people.

When slave Jacob wrote his complete name, he used "Fontaine" as his last name since it was his owner's name. Jacob Fontaine's first job in the church in 1855 was that of sexton at his master's St. David's Episcopal Church in Austin. At the age of 47, Jacob Fontaine had the responsibility of maintaining the church property. As Fontaine worked in the sanctuary, he must have felt God calling him to preach. Knowing that there were other denominations he had experienced as a child, the want-to-be preacher reached out to other churches.

He tried to hear sermons from different Christian ministers, so in 1860, he attended the First Baptist Church in Austin. While sitting in the back row with other black worshipers, he met an interesting older white man who slipped into the back pew late sometimes. He met Sam Houston.

While working for the Espiscopalian minister, Edward Fontaine, Jacob cleaned the church in the morning and slipped over to the basement of an old Methodist church at Brazos and Tenth Streets in the afternoon.

Jacob Fontaine, once a slave, preached in the Austin area, owned several businesses and printed a newspaper, the Gold Dollar. *Courtesy of Austin History Center, Austin Public Library.*

In this dimly lit room below the street level, he preached to a black congregation. Some of these black Christians longed for a church of their own, so they began to meet secretly to plan such an endeavor.

Jacob Fontaine and his followers were able to see that dream come true in 1867. They established the First Colored Baptist Church in Austin at that time. Emancipation was in full swing, and fifty-nine-year-old Fontaine had his own church to pastor. At this time, he involved himself with many jobs as if he was afraid he would miss doing something that came his way.

While preaching at his new church, Fontaine was janitor at the old Land Office Building. The influence of his former owner, Edward Fontaine, in politics piqued his desire to be a part of that scene also. Eventually Jacob Fontaine became active in the Republican and Greenback parties during the Reconstruction days. But preaching and politics were not all that entertained Fontaine's mind. He and his family operated a grocery, laundry, book and medicine store. The Fontaine household sold all these products and washed their client's clothes under one roof.

Another interest of Fontaine's was getting information and news disseminated to the black community. In 1876 Fontaine produced the Austin *Gold Dollar*, one of the first black weekly newspapers in the South. In 1872, Fontaine returned to Mississippi and visited his sister. The siblings had been separated due to slavery for twenty years. She gave him a gold dollar during the visit, and he later made an investment with the coin. From the money made on the gold piece, he had enough cash to start his newspaper, aptly named the *Gold Dollar*.

By 1867 Fontaine emerged as a leader in the black community. At that time he helped establish the St. John Regular Missionary Baptist Association and was elected its moderator. He was also a circuit rider of sorts because this position propelled him about the area visiting black communities and founding new churches. He established the Mount Zion Church in Williamson Creek, in 1873; Good Hope Church in Round Rock, in 1874; Sweet Home Church in Clarksville in 1877; New Hope Church in Wheatsville in 1887; and St. Stephen's Church in Waters Park in 1887.

While Fontaine printed his newspaper, ran his store and started new churches, he was no young whippersnapper. He undertook this whirlwind of activities in his late seventies and early eighties.

Even though some of Jacob and Melvina Fontaine's early jobs were as servants, that fact brought about some interesting connections for the family in later years. When their daughter Melissa married a custodian, Joe Gordon, March 18, 1870, the wedding took place in the Governor's Mansion. Melvina Fontaine worked for the Governor and his wife, so they offered their home for the special event. The Fontaine family included two other daughters and a son.

By the year 1875, the Fontaines lived in a two-story house at 24th and Orange. The parson, always looking for another cause to pursue, advocated in 1881 that a university be built in the Austin area. He spoke out for the college and became Austin's leading black advocate for the establishment of the University of Texas at Austin. Again he hit the road for a cause as he traveled to San Antonio, Sequin and Marlin urging black people to vote for the university.

The Fontaines continued to live on the corner of Orange Street until Jacob died in 1898 at the age of ninety. Their home is now a landmark in Austin.

Jacob Fontaine's work continued under the watchful eye of his son George. Here was another man who balanced several jobs at one time. He worked as a depot porter in Austin while he carried on his father's church work and newspaper publishing. George had a new name for his publication in 1897–1898. He called it the *Silver Messenger*. Jacob Fontaine had a grandson who also continued the Fontaine tradition. Rev. Israel Jacob Fontaine III founded the Fontaine Memorial Baptist Church in 1962 and published the Austin *Express* and the Fort Worth *Community News*. Grandson Jacob also went into advertising and insurance work.

When Jacob Fontaine came to Austin in 1839, he might have bumped into another slave destined to lead his people spiritually, Nace Duval. In the 1840s, Duval brought together a large group of black Methodists with whom he shared the Bible. He would teach them the word of God and exhort them to live Christian lives. When Duval ministered to people, he worked with white as well as black believers. At one time, Duval teamed with Rev. Homer S. Thrall to visit church members in the area around Austin. Thrall discussed Duval's leadership ability when he said, "He had considerable influence with the whites, and with his assistance, we built a small house of worship for the Negroes."

Although Fontaine spent most of his life around Austin, Duval left the area after emancipation. He continued to do the Lord's work in different places. Duval built a church for black people of San Antonio and passed away as a man loved by many.

Of all the Negro preachers who made it out of the South and came to Texas, none wanted his freedom more badly than Matthew Gaines. He knew the first skill he needed to have in order to survive in the free world was the ability to read. Born in Pineville, near Alexandria, Louisiana, August 4, 1840, Matthew Gaines had a hunger for knowledge. He often trudged up the road near his family's cabin to see another lad. A white boy living on the same plantation that Matthew did became his friend. As Gaines expressed his desire to read, his white friend smuggled books to him. The plantation owner's son helped him learn to read as they looked at the books by candlelight. Learning the printed page made Matthew more intent on freedom. This newfound ability gave him courage.

To prove his determination to be on his own, Gaines ran away from his owner twice. At twelve years of age, he was sold to a man from Louisiana. His new owner hired him out as a laborer on a steamboat. Gaines thought this would be an excellent chance to run away, so he made a dash for freedom. Or maybe it was a splash for freedom as he left the boat. He made it to Camden, Arkansas, stayed there for six months and walked to New Orleans.

By this time Gaines probably thought he was free for good. His new home of New Orleans had thousands of residents, so surely he could blend in with everybody else. However, his freedom was short lived. Gaines was caught and returned to his master.

When Gaines reached the age of twenty-three, a planter in Robertson County, Texas, owned him. He still hated the life of a slave even if he was in Texas, so he made plans to run away. Gaines knew he was strong and smart enough to escape successfully, so he left his home heading south. His plan was to travel through remote West Texas and make it to Mexico. However, he did not count on the troopers at Fort McKavett, Menard County, catching him.

As he neared the fort, the soldiers captured him. This time he was returned to his owner near Fredericksburg. He resigned himself to be a better worker since his attempts to leave had failed. The two or so years before emancipation, Gaines learned blacksmithing and how to care for sheep as a herder. But the minute he was free, he left his old life behind and headed toward Burton in Washington County. This time when he walked down the road, nobody stopped him. It was a good feeling.

Gaines began to preach, possibly for the first time. As he talked to the church members on Sunday and listened to their concerns, he realized that black people looked up to him as a leader of their community. Reconstruction days opened up the possibility of black men running for office, and this chance intrigued the young preacher. Gaines ran for the senate and was elected a senator of the Sixteenth District of the Texas Legislature. In this capacity, he had the chance to speak out for the rights and interests of his own black people, and he did. His concerns included education, prison reform, the protection of blacks at the polls, the election of blacks to public office and tenant-farming reform.

When he listened to his church members on Sunday, he heard about some blacks being mistreated in jail, and some blacks not getting a fair share of their crops as they worked as tenant farmers.

Gaines felt that religious, as well as educational groups would improve educational opportunities for all people, if these groups did not have to pay taxes. He wanted also to exempt buildings and equipment that belonged to these organizations. Gaines jumped up and down with joy as he told his people that the bill passed June 12, 1871.

This preacher had watched mob violence sweep over inmates who could not be protected in a real jail, so his next bit of legislation addressed that issue. When this bill passed, he was successful in getting a new jail constructed in his district. The third bill he helped to pass was the Militia Bill. This legislation protected blacks as well as everybody at the voting booth.

Gaines' successful tenure as a politician was cut short when he was convicted of bigamy in 1873 and was not allowed to complete his six-year term in the senate. This charge was later overturned, and he was re-elected. A strange thing happened: the Democratic white majority seated his opponent instead. Even though he was upset, Gaines continued to expound on his political views. He used conventions, public gatherings and his pulpit to voice his thoughts for the black people. He died in 1900 in Giddings.

One black Texas preacher had a very different past than the slaves who came to Texas. Israel S. Campbell hopped about among several states with his church work. Israel, born in Russellville, Kentucky, in 1815, joined the Baptist Church as a twenty-one-year-old and began preaching soon after. He had the freedom and finances to travel as a preacher to Tennessee, Canada and Ohio. Israel Campbell was officially ordained as a minister in Canada in 1855.

Although it looked as if he found a home in the country north of the United States, Campbell unexpectedly returned to the South. He had his headquarters in Baton Rouge and served as a general missionary to Baptists in Louisiana. Just when he seemed to have a nice life in his new home, the Baptist Convention met in Nashville, Tennessee, in 1866. They decided to send him where they thought missionaries were needed most. They sent him to Texas.

Campbell did not waste much time unpacking before he, with the help of pastor I. Rhinehart, organized the Antioch Baptist Church in Houston a few months after the convention sent him to Texas. He preached at that church until John Henry Yates was ordained and selected as resident pastor.

Campbell moved down the coast a bit and developed the African Baptist Church in Galveston. In its creation year, 1867, it was the first independent black Baptist church formed in Texas after emancipation. This roving preacher decided to stay awhile in Galveston and work with this congregation. While he brought the sermons there on Sunday morning, his congregation swelled from forty-seven to 500 members.

Campbell helped other churches in the area, and they formed the Regular Missionary Lincoln Baptist Association. Since Campbell had been moderator of Baptist associations in Michigan and Louisiana and president of the Freedman's Baptist Convention for two years, his leadership skills were obvious to anyone observing him speak. He was selected first moderator of the Lincoln Association, which was the first association of black Baptists in Texas.

Campbell's new responsibilities were similar to his missionary work as a youth. Now he had twenty churches to visit that were scattered from south of Galveston to north along the Brazos River to McLennan County. After four years, Campbell and others decided the group needed to organize a formal, statewide organization. He wrote the constitution for the Baptist State Missionary Convention in 1872.

Campbell looked over his church members and realized that there were many of them that could benefit from vocational training. He set about trying to get a vocational school organized in his area. He wanted to pattern it after the one developed by Booker T. Washington. However, a group in Marshall, Texas, had another idea. Bishop College, established in 1881, was supported by the Baptist Church and planned to teach academic and non-vocational subjects. He laid his plans aside to support this new institution.

By the year 1890, Campbell felt his age and health required him to go at a slower pace. His daughter, Mary, invited him to live with her family. Israel Campbell was now 75 years old and ready for retirement. Mary married James Henry Washington, a member of the Texas House of

Representatives. They lived in La Marque on a farm when Israel Campbell came to live with them. The family grew vegetables for sale on a truck farm and raised chickens. The following year, Campbell officially retired from his beloved First Regular Missionary Baptist Church in Galveston. His connection with them spanned some twenty-four years. The old workhorse was turned out to pasture but not forgotten. At that time people called him the "Father of black Baptists in Texas." He died in La Marque on June 13, 1898, and was buried in Lakeview Cemetery, Galveston.

Many Negro preachers spread the gospel in Texas even though the roads they traveled were bumpy. A man who preached the gospel from Central Texas to El Paso, L. R. Millican, also traveled some rough roads of West Texas.

6

BROTHER L. R. MILLICAN:
1853–1925

L eander Randon Millican, born in 1853, grew up in Texas too young
to wear the South's gray uniform but old enough as a seven-year-old
to watch Confederate troopers march at nearby Camp Speight. Millican
daydreamed about battles they would someday fight as he listened to
their clanging swords and booming cannon fire.

Millican, born August 27, 1853, lived in the town called Millican in
Brazos County. His parents, Elliot McNeil and Marcella Elizabeth Milli-
can, lived on a land grant in that area given to Elliot's father. The older
Millican was part of Austin's Three Hundred Colonists.

During the Civil War, most able-bodied men were gone, so young-
sters had to perform jobs normally done by the adults. As a busy eight-
year-old, Leander (or L. R.) Millican delivered important documents to
nearby county seats. With legs not long enough to use his daddy's stir-
rups, he bounced along on a horse. He rode sixteen miles on some trips
while holding tightly to his legal documents.

About two years later, Millican's world came apart when his father
died, his mother remarried, and his older brothers went off to war. At
that time, he found himself all alone and had to grow up fast.

As a lanky teenager, Millican carried the mail between Lampasas
and Austin. He rode a little Spanish mule, which was not built for speed.
However, when attacked by Indians, he and the mule managed to escape
the arrows whizzing by. Millican decided the mail delivery business was
too calm a way of life, so he moved farther west and signed on to cowboy a spell for a big cow outfit.

By the age of eighteen, Millican returned to Lampasas and served all
the papers that Justice of the Peace Captain Pratt had to have dispersed.

During that time, a quick-draw gunslinger named Lou Sawyers came to Lampasas with the sole intent to cause trouble. His friend Rogers was in jail waiting to be tried the next day.

Katy Stokes in *Paisano—Story of a Cowboy and a Camp Meeting* explained how Millican was pulled into being a lawman. Some of the good citizens of the town were armed to the teeth because they did not want Lou Sawyer to help his friend or shoot up the town. The deputy sheriff could see trouble brewing, so he asked for somebody to help him. When no one stepped forward, and silence stretched out as long as a stake rope, Millican quietly said, "I'll go."

The deputy replied, "You don't know what you're doing, young fellow!" Eventually the lawman had no other takers, so he told Millican to get his gun and come on. When they approached the gunslinger, Millican began to pass the time of day with him. Sawyer was asked to give up his gun, but he did not want to. Millican spoke to him in a calm voice and said, "Mr. Lou, do you see that crowd of old men over there? Well, they and the group at the store just beyond have made up their minds that there shall be no more trouble here if it can be avoided."

Sawyer waited awhile and told Millican that he would leave his gun with Uncle Weaver at the saloon. The two men made it through the rest of Lou's stay in town without a shot being fired.

Town officials did not forget Millican's bravery against Lou Sawyer, so they bestowed the title of Justice of the Peace on him. In 1874, he was twenty-one years old, old enough to be elected deputy sheriff of Lampasas County.

His quiet but firm way of handling hoodlums amazed a lot of people. One time, L. R. Millican was on a train when a rowdy, drunken codger boarded and started shooting his guns. When Millican asked the conductor to control the dangerous man, the trainman replied that the gunman was too mean to try to stop. The conductor suggested they wait until the train pulled into a town that had a lawman.

Millican said, "Well, I will do something about it myself, as I am not going to let some drunk man frighten these women and children any longer." The next time the drunk came through Millican's coach, he grabbed the man's shoulders and threw him into a nearby seat. Quietly, but in a firm voice, he told the rowdy character to settle down and quit bothering folks. To everybody's surprise, the man obeyed Millican and sat rather subdued the rest of the trip.

A profound event took place in Millican's life in the summer of 1874. He went to a District Methodist Camp Meeting on Cherokee Creek in San Saba County. He had been disinterested in religion up to this point, but suddenly the preacher's words made sense, and that night he was converted. Millican studied the scriptures at length the next few months and felt a call to preach.

He was baptized a Baptist on a cold December day, and immediately entered Baylor University to learn to preach. He threw his deputy sheriff's badge away and hit the books. Although Millican tried to meet classes daily, his stay in college was brief. Baylor University records do not show Millican as a student after 1875, so the open country called him more than the classroom did.

As the young circuit rider guided his horse to various homes in Lampasas County, he was acutely aware that the Horrell family frequently shot up the area and stole livestock. Millican already knew this information because he had met the Horrells face to face as he held the job of deputy sheriff. Finally the state police, who were ordered to squelch the violence during Reconstruction Days, decided they had better pay a visit to Lampasas County.

Policeman Capt. Thomas Williams had seven men riding with him to stop the Horrell brothers: Mart, Tom, Merritt, Ben and Sam. When the smoke settled in Jerry Scott's saloon, four policemen were dead. Mart Horrell, severely wounded, was removed to the Georgetown jail.

However, his stay was short as his brothers decided he needed other accommodations. They broke him out of confinement. After so much turmoil, this "genteel" family finally decided to move to Ruidoso, New Mexico. But their new neighbors did not seem to appreciate them any more in New Mexico than the old ones did in Texas. The Horrells initiated a bloody battle called the Horrell War in New Mexico, so authorities chased them back to Texas in a short time.

In order to be good citizens of their hometown, the brothers surrendered to Lampasas authorities. The Horrells were acquitted of the death of Thomas Williams a year before, so they were determined to live in peace.

One day young Millican stopped in the Lampasas area to visit a business. When he returned to the place where he tied his horse, the animal was gone. Millican went straight to the hideout of the Horrells and told them about his missing horse. The leader of the gang walked around their camp and returned to tell Millican, "Yes, I see your horse is here. I'll have it ready for you in a few minutes."

The Horrell brothers could not live peacefully very long even though they were back in Lampasas County. For two years they quarreled with Pinckney Calhoun (Pink) Higgins who stated flat out that they were stealing his cattle. The Horrells considered Higgins a neighbor before they began feuding. Now accusations shot between the two factions and ill will continued. Finally on January 22, 1877, Pink Higgins killed Merritt Horrell in Wiley's and Toland's Gem Saloon in Lampasas. Some observers think it was the same saloon where the four state policemen died earlier in a Horrell brothers fight. .

The Horrells planned to make Higgins pay in blood, but Pink Higgins did not give them time to organize. He recruited his brother-in-law Bob Mitchell and his friend Bill Wren. Pink Higgins's gang took matters into their hands again as they waylaid Tom and Mart Horrell March 26, 1877. These two men were on their way to attend a session of Judge W. A. Blackburn's court. Tom was shot out of the saddle and hurt badly, but his brother chased off the Higgins group with heavy gunfire.

On June 6, 1877, both the Higgins's gang and the Horrell brothers met accidentally in Lampasas. This chance meeting occurred after somebody mysteriously broke into the Lampasas Courthouse and destroyed the district records. These lost papers just happened to be the bonds of Pink Higgins and his friend Bob Mitchell. Gunfire sang out from both groups in the town's streets, and this time the wounds were much worse. Bill Wren had a bad injury, and Frank Mitchell, Bob's brother, died. Jim Buck Miller, a recent addition to the Horrell gang, lay lifeless also.

How this feud finally ended is a story with two possible endings. Some Texas Rangers under Maj. John B. Jones's command awakened the Horrells one morning not so gently. The officers arrested them and had the Horrells, along with the Higginses, sign a statement that the feud was over. This document is still in the Adjutant General's papers.

Gunfire ceased in the county between the two families, and neighbors thought the outlawing factions had mended their ways. However, some people believed that Tom and Mart Horrell were involved in one more caper in Bosque County. In 1878, somebody robbed a country store and murdered the proprietor in that area. Lawmen cornered the Horrell brothers who soon found themselves sitting in a Meridian jail cell. Vigilantes had their own trial and shot the two outlaws.

Since Millican kept abreast of the events that occurred in Lampasas County, as well as the adjoining area, he knew the two fighting groups quite well. When he was preaching in the same county, a member of one of the gangs died, and gang members asked Millican to preach his funeral. After the ceremony was over, several of the gang asked Millican to walk away from the crowd with them. An ordinary man would have wondered what mischief they meant to do, but Millican went with them. The spokesman for the group explained how they knew they could make things right with their neighbors, but they wanted a way to wipe out the past and get a new start.

Millican preached the gospel to them and told the outlaws that they did have hope. Some of the gunslingers became Christians, and the preacher watched their families develop into law-abiding citizens. All was not lost in the Horrell-Higgins feud, but as far as anyone knew, Millican never converted Pink Higgins.

When the smoking guns cooled off in Lampasas, Higgins decided to move to the Panhandle area with his wife, Lena, and their family. He settled around the community of Spur where he became known as a cattleman and rancher. Before he hardly unpacked his saddlebags, the area people found that he handled a .44 pistol and his Winchester quite well. He wiped out some cattle thieves. Since all the ranchers shared this problem, the Espuela Land & Cattle Company hired Higgins to keep rustlers away from Spur steers in 1900.

The locals began to respect this man with unequaled nerve. He could fire either the pistol or the rifle with deadly aim. Word was that Pink Higgins earned his pay. When rustlers even suspected he was in their area, they hurriedly changed occupations or locations.

Even though Higgins was known for his hard tactics with rustlers, he loved his family. He was absent from home for weeks at a time, a fact that worried him. His neighbors decided to help the Higgins family when he was away from his ranch. Area cowboys rode by the Higgins home regularly to check on Lena and the kids. One cold Sunday morning, Higgins visited the Methodist tabernacle where a revival was taking place. Some church members were a bit surprised when tough, burly Higgins walked the sawdust trail and accepted Christ as his Savior. That was one time when he left the .44 at home.

While Higgins departed from Lampasas to live in the Panhandle, Millican moved also. In September 1879, Millican was commissioned as missionary for the San Saba Association at a salary that some thought was too high at $35 a month. He first worked with small churches around Lampasas. After a while, he included Burnet and Llano in his circuit.

Life was never tame for Millican. He would break a bronc to ride and then have to swim swollen streams to get to the next church. Once he and his horse got into the Colorado River when it was raging with floodwaters. The swirling water took him under a steep overhanging bluff that had whirlpools tugging at him and his horse. Finally, Millican swam downstream enough to get out.

Ten years later, he got into trouble in the same river. He had been holding meetings and distributing Bibles with an old Baylor classmate, F. S. Rountree. They separated, and Millican was alone as he drove two horses pulling a hack into the water. As soon as he realized the whole rig was going to be swept away, he tried to cut loose the horses. The footbrake caught his boot, which he could not loosen. As the hack turned over in the water, Millican was trapped underneath. Just before he drowned, he was able to pull his boot off and wiggle to the surface. The hack and one horse were lost in the river. Millican had to ride to town with one horse and one boot.

If almost drowning was not scary enough for the preacher, Millican also had an encounter with Indians who still roamed the Davis Mountain area. He was riding alone while returning from Fort Davis. A scouting party of Indians attacked him at Barrell Springs. Millican took off as fast as his mare would go and fired a shot every now and then at the Indians. Luckily for him, the parson ran into a bunch of cowboys. Suddenly the Indians decided the chase was over.

After the ordeal, Millican explained the action. He said, "I run. I had a little black mare that was mighty fast, and I urged her to do her best." Millican had a lot of nerve traveling alone because it was common knowledge among the Fort Davis soldiers that no one should go more than three or four miles from the fort. That warning included soldiers who hunted alone.

Millican's first Sweetwater Association sprawled over four hundred miles. His second Association was almost as large, for it encompassed territory from around San Angelo all the way to El Paso.

To get around such a large area, Millican rode the trains to his new preaching area in 1888. He also rode the first car he got ahold of a lot like he did his horses: "as fast as it would run." However, he did treat cars a lot like horses. One man rode with him up a high hill and noticed the preacher killed the motor at the summit. The fellow asked Millican why they stopped. He said, "Gotta let this engine cool." In his mind he was still riding a horse that needed a breather after a hard climb.

Leander Randon "L. R." Millican was a deputy sheriff, cattleman and Baptist preacher. Courtesy of Paisano Baptist Encampment, Alpine, Texas.

While L. R. Millican rode horses, cars or trains to get around the Davis Mountains and the huge open spaces around El Paso, he met another circuit rider making the same trails. Rev. William Benjamin Bloys came to the Fort Davis area in 1888 hoping its dry climate would help his lung problems. He brought with him a wife and three little children, but he brought them to a far different place than the home they left behind.

William Bloys, born January 26, 1847, at McLemoresville, Tennessee, must have thought the Civil War broke out in his own back yard. His saddle-making father, Mordecai Bloys, believed in the Union and had to move the family to Illinois in 1862, for fear of his neighbor's reprisal. Most of Tennessee stood strongly for the Confederates. Young Bloys was schooled in a Salem academy before he settled into ten years as a teacher and farmer. Later he entered Lane Theological Seminary in Cincinnati at the age of twenty-nine. He planned to be a Presbyterian foreign missionary when he graduated in 1879. Soon after seminary days were over, Bloys married Isabelle Catherine Veck.

He practically had his bags packed for overseas as he planned to preach to the sinners in some exotic place like India. However, Bloys's delicate health changed his plans. A lung ailment shut the doors to any possibility of being accepted to a foreign post. Bloys was not to be denied some form of missionary work, so he applied to the Presbyterian Home Mission Program. They accepted him, and he was soon on the road with his family to a spot called Coleman, Texas, in 1879.

This new mission might not have been so different from India because Bloys had no church house in which to say his prayers. The first time he opened the Good Book to the people in that town, it was in a room precariously situated over the saloon. His circuit included preaching opportunities in towns like Runnels, Buffalo Gap and Santa Anna. After riding on this circuit for months, Bloys's work paid off as he developed churches in several of these communities.

The parson often comforted the sick as he prayed for them in their homes. He had served in the Coleman area for eight years when he moved from one sick bed to another in terribly cold, wet weather. The Reverend Bloys came down with a bad case of pneumonia, the kind his weak lungs did not need. He spent many days in bed. After he slowly improved a bit, his doctor recommended a higher altitude. Bloys received a letter from a friend, David Merrill, who told him about the need for a preacher in Fort Davis, a town near his son Jesse W. Merrill's ranch. Bloys gladly accepted the invite.

Not long after settling into his new home and visiting the town of Fort Davis, Bloys met some rough characters. Cowboys frequented the eleven saloons in this tiny town near the fort. Shooting up the streets and gurgling down the booze seemed to be their main occupation. Often, the Texas Rangers had to make their appearance before court could be held in the nearby courthouse.

However, William Bloys did not seem to be intimidated by the rough atmosphere of this place. Instead, he became pastor of the First Presbyterian Church at Fort Davis, which also included the job of ministering to people wherever they lived in the surrounding Davis Mountains.

This Presbyterian minister preached in cow camps, homes or anywhere a few people wanted to hear the Bible read. Bloys also tied his horse regularly at the hitching rail at nearby Fort Davis and voluntarily served as chaplain at that post until it closed in 1891.

The First Presbyterian Church of Fort Davis, situated on Bloys Avenue with the Davis Mountains in the background, was a church where Reverend William Bloys preached. Photo courtesy of Sharon Gentry.

Fort Davis, established in 1857, was visited often by Reverend William Bloys. Photo courtesy of Sharon Gentry.

During this time, preachers like L. R. Millican and William Bloys of Fort Davis knew they could not see everybody in the Davis Mountain region by riding around their circuit. Some ranches were a hundred miles apart. Ranch families rarely got to worship with others, so a camp meeting seemed like a good way to bring everybody together. After friends and cowboys encouraged Bloys to have such a gathering, he preached while the first coffee pot heated at the chuckwagon on October 10, 1890.

Ranch families enjoyed the food and fellowship, as well as the sermon. Forty-three people came to this first meeting under the sprawling live oak trees near Fort Davis. The men of the camp erected a brush arbor for some of the next meetings and later used a big tent, which very well could have come from nearby Fort Davis army inventory.

A shady area called Skillman's Grove, about sixteen miles southwest of Fort Davis, was the site for this gathering. Bloys got along well with Millican and other preachers, so this camp meeting included Presbyterians, Methodists, Baptists and Disciples of Christ. Ranch families studied the Bible and heard preaching for two days at these first get-togethers.

By 1912, the camp had a tabernacle. Although Bloys directed the camp, Millican worked at this cowboy meeting from the time it started and helped in any way possible.

Many of the cowboys who came to the services had never been in church before, even though they were thirty or forty years old. One particular cowboy found the Lord at a night service, and after most of the crowd went to bed, he was talking to the other men around the campfire. He said he had to leave to get back to his outfit, but he wanted to be baptized that night.

Millican had gone to bed early. The men remembered that the old preacher always said, "I'll baptize you any time, anywhere," so they woke him up for the ceremony. The parson threw a slicker over himself, grabbed a lantern and headed to the nearby creek. When the cowboy and the preacher walked into the river, they noticed it was up a bit from the rains that night, and a few hailstones floating along the top of the water made it ice-cold. However, Millican never winced; he just walked further out into the water with his slicker on, baptized the fellow and watched the new convert dry off. The baptized Christian commenced his twenty-mile ride back to his cow camp because he had to be ready to work at daybreak the next day.

Frail Rev. Bloys, who led the Cowboy Camp Meeting all these years, died in 1917, so the group at Skillman's Grove decided to name their gathering Bloys Camp Meeting. The people asked Millican to be temporary chairman for meetings in 1917. "Temporary status" has a way of extending, and the group named Millican "temporary chairman" for three years. The meeting in August, now called the Bloys Encampment, had unusual visitors in 1919 – U. S. soldiers from nearby Canderalia on the Rio Grande.

A group of U. S. soldiers were camped along the Rio Grande at Canderalia because border bandits had the ranchers of the area worried. Some lone ranch houses had received unwanted visitors looking for loot. This Canderalia outpost was a little over 50 miles from the Bloys Encampment, and one incident along the border affected the camp members. On August 10, 1919, a DH-4 plane left Marfa, about 21 miles southwest of Fort Davis, to fly a routine border patrol flight with a crew of Lt. H. G. Peterson, the pilot, and Lt. Paul H. Davis, the observer-gunner. The two men flew over Presidio, Texas, and mistook the swollen Rio Conchos, which flows into the Rio Grande at Oji-naga, for the Rio Grande. Unknowingly, pilots Peterson and Davis flew accidentally into Mexico's airspace.

After flying two hours, the men noticed landmarks that were not on their map. When their rigging on one wing gave way, they crashed on top of a mesa. As they crawled from the wreckage, they saw barren land every direction they looked. There were no houses in view or men to rescue them. Peterson and Davis checked their legs and bodies for scratches, but the few bumps here and there produced little pain.

Since the airmen were unharmed, they started walking toward the border. In the first few hours of their journey, they emptied their can-teen. Soon they became very thirsty, tired and scratched by the brush and cacti. Suddenly several Mexican men riding horseback appeared, and the pilots thought they were rescued. Instead, the riders circled the pilots, and the two men found themselves looking down a rifle barrel. A one-legged bandit named Jesus Renteria and his gang captured the two young men. This border bandit knew how to make money. He quickly sent word to a Capt. Leonard Matlock who had U. S. troops stationed at Candelaria and demanded $15,000 ransom money for the two aviators.

When Matlock wired the U. S. Government in Washington for the money, they could not get it to Texas by the August 19 deadline that Renteria had imposed. After racking their brain trying to think who had money, the troopers went to the Bloys Encampment, which was in ses-sion that week. In a short time, the soldiers received pledges from the ranchers there to get the full $15,000 from the First National Bank of Marfa and deliver it to Capt. Matlock. On August 18, H. N. Fennell of the Marfa National Bank, along with an Eighth Cavalry Officer, brought the money to where Captain Matlock and his troops were camped. That afternoon Matlock rode to the village of San Antonio and showed agents of Renteria that he indeed did have the money.

The outlaw holding the two flyers wanted Matlock to meet him quite a few miles into the interior of Mexico, but the soldier refused. Matlock decided that this scenario would make it too easy for the ban-dits to kill him as well as the aviators. As time ran out and August 19 ar-rived, Matlock forced Renteria to bring the hostages to the border at a little town called San Antonio. The two men agreed to exchange the prisoners and money at midnight. Matlock volunteered to take the money across the Rio Grande and get the hostages one at a time, but he told the outlaws that if anything happed to the hostages, he would charge his troops into the little town and kill everybody. The captain made no idle threat; he meant to fulfill his bluff because he had two hundred troopers waiting nearby in the darkness that night to attack at his signal.

Matlock, riding alone, crossed the bridge, met the outlaws' representative and exchanged half the money for Peterson. With the aviator riding behind Matlock, the first prisoner made it back to safety. Matlock left Peterson on U. S. soil and returned across the Rio Grande to pick up Davis. On his second trip, nobody stepped out to meet him at the designated meeting place. Matlock waited until finally he saw the Mexican guard and Davis coming out of a nearby cornfield.

Davis walked in front of the bandit. When the prisoner came near, Matlock whispered for him to jump up on the horse. Matlock pulled out a pistol and told the bandit he would kill him if necessary, but that he would not give him the rest of the money. Matlock whirled his horse in the direction of American soil and delivered his prisoner safely across the border. The Captain also saved the U. S. Government some money.

The Bloys Encampment ranchers got their $15,000 eventually from the U. S. Government. For this particular challenge, the good Christians helped get the bad guys.

Millican had been warned about such bandits as he rode alone over the Big Bend countryside. People would admonish him to be careful because bandits roamed the same country that the preacher did. Millican would say that none of the Mexicans would hurt him. This fact was probably true because even the treacherous outlaws would not bother a man of God. The Mexican families taught their children from an early age to be respectful to the Catholic padres, and this attitude extended to include lone circuit riders like Millican.

There was one hitch to this theory of the parson's. If a lone bandit saw a rider a great distance away, he might shoot the man of God before he knew his identity. By 1915, the Mexicans had fought in the revolution so long that few horses were available. Any bandit knew he could turn a horse and saddle into good money. Lone riders like the preacher were at risk of receiving a bullet.

L. R. Millican spent many hours in the saddle as he rode the circuit of the Davis Mountains. He constantly made plans for a Baptist encampment in those hills. Although he enjoyed helping with the Bloys Encampment, his dream visualized a gathering for the Baptist brethren. Finally he resigned his post as leader of the Bloys Encampment because his dream became a reality; there was a Baptist encampment across the mountains in Madera Canyon. About a hundred people, hungry for the gospel, drove their buggies up the canyon floor to hear preaching in 1902.

Since Millican was appointed a missionary for the Big Bend area, all these mountains were his home. He worked with other preachers, and the next Baptist encampment had 500 people to hear the well-known Baptist, Bro. George Truett, speak. This well-loved preacher stood in a wagon and explained how God loves all sinners. As the camp grew larger, Millican and others looked for land that would be more accessible for a large crowd. Not all plans went so well with the new camp because some years there was no camp meeting at all. Then World War I came, and even preachers like Truett were asked to speak to the troops instead of cowboys in the Davis Mountains.

When Millican thought his dream of a Baptist encampment would never be a reality, the year 1921 proved him wrong. At that time, a meeting place at Paisano Pass, a community near a railroad track that could bring people from long distances, became available. This location was between Alpine and Marfa, about equal distance from each. Millican's dream materialized as the night air in July carried sounds of "On Jordan's Stormy Banks" and "Amazing Grace." Paisano Baptist Encampment had people praising God and saying amen to the preaching. This encampment is still active today.

Another group of Christian believers camped on the banks of the South Concho River just south of San Angelo in Tom Green County. In the late 1800s, all the churches in this community of Christoval had a revival together. The location for this get together was a brush arbor. Rancher W. C. Jones remembered a time when not all the events at the revival were serious as he explained an interruption caused by a couple of young Christoval citizens.

These two teenage boys, supposed to be front-and-center sitting in a pew, managed to slip out of the tabernacle and stand in the darkness nearby while the preacher spoke. The lanterns hung around the building cast light inside where worshippers sat but did not illuminate the area outside the tabernacle. The boys hid in the darkness.

Paisano Baptist Encampment, between Alpine and Marfa, was started by L. R. Millican. Paisano Peak, showing in the background, marks the location of this camp. Author's collection.

As the preacher spoke loudly urging his audience to repent of sin, so they could go to heaven, one lady jumped up from her seat. She shouted loudly, "Lord, I'm coming home." She continued to look upward into the brush arbor above her and say, "Lord, I'm coming home." About that time, the two boys got an idea. An old hound dog slept near their feet. They grabbed him by his big, floppy ears and threw him on top of the brush arbor. As the excited lady looked up to heaven, the dog fell through the brush arbor and hit her. Quite a commotion ensued, and it took some time before worship could resume.

In later years, the people of the Christoval area wanted to worship at a Baptist camp meeting much like Millican's encampment further west. Billie Marie Van Court attended this Christoval Baptist Encampment in the 1920s and 1930s. She described what it was like.

She said "The preachin' was great and the singin' lifted you to heaven, but as a child the fireflies dipping around the water's edge also caught my attention." Billie explained that they brought all of Mom's yummy canned vegetables, plus some pulled fresh from the garden just before they left.

Each family had its own makeshift refrigerator—a block of ice, buried and covered with sacks to cool the food stacked around it.

Fresh meat would not keep long in the hot sun, so some campers brought their meat still alive. The campers stuffed frying-sized chickens in a coop and brought them on the wagon or back of a Model T Ford. When mealtime rolled around, mothers would remove a chicken from the coop and wring its neck. The next thing campers heard was the crackling sound of the chicken cooking in the frying pan.

Everyone threw bedrolls in the car, and if people were lucky, they had a tent to take along. They were used mostly as a place to change clothes. With the hot sun bearing down on that tent, campers had a sauna experience by the time they changed into church-going attire called "day clothes." All the girls primped in front of a mirror that Mother remembered to bring from the front bedroom and hang on a tree limb.

Billie Marie said that mirror got a lot of use. The men used it for shaving, and the girls walked by it to see if any boys were following them.

Different people brought different supplies for the weeklong stay. A rancher might bring his chuck wagon to help feed his brood. Most campers slept on cots, but the older campers did not feel comfortable in such small beds. These "senior citizens" brought their iron bedsteads from home and slept out under the stars.

For most children, the favorite time of the day was swim time. Female swimming attire consisted of bloomers that reached to the knees and tops that covered their arms to the elbows. Females had to swim at allotted places for "girls only." Those cute guys had to swim at other times. The water in the Concho River that flowed through the town of Christoval was cool, so everybody had a great time splashing in it.

The older boys in camp had a special job; they had to carry drinking water from the springs on the south side of the river. Girls managed to show up at the springs about the same time the boys were filling buckets. If a girl got too close to the operation, the boys would throw snakes or frogs at her.

Two large pavilions sprawled over the campgrounds. Their main floor was for Bible study classes, and the second story was a place where the visiting preacher and camp personnel could stay. Presidents of the major Baptist colleges attended the encampment and recruited students for the coming year.

Women swam at different times than the men did at the Christoval Baptist Encampment on the South Concho River in Christoval, Texas. Courtesy of the West Texas Collection at Angelo State University, San Angelo, Texas.

In the 1920s, if a student said he had no money for tuition, the administrator told the young person to come to college anyway. Many a student worked in the cafeteria or at another campus job and paid his way through college during the 1920s and 1930s. One of the lady campers was a good piano teacher. When she found out that some of the young people there were interested in playing piano, she gave lessons in the afternoon when the instrument was not in use for worship service.

Christoval was so pleased to have the big crowd of visitors each summer that a newspaper, *Christoval Baptist Encampment News,* was published. A young high school student named Grady Hill published this one-page paper every day. Visitors thought of him as a tall, gangly boy, but he enjoyed a prestigious career in journalism later in life.

This encampment, near San Angelo, Texas, drew the largest crowds of any gathering of its kind. President E. F. Lyon spoke proudly in 1922 when he said, "We had the distinction last year of having the largest encampment held in the United States."

To get an accurate count of attendees was difficult, though. The large tabernacle held only about 2,200 people. Many worshippers sat outside under the pecan trees and listened to the sermons. Among the well-known preachers who spoke along the Concho River were George W. Truett and R. G. Lee. These men could "pack the pew," so many people felt that the numbers swelled to at least 5,000 or maybe even 8,000 to 10,000 through the 1920s.

Such an encampment would go on forever, or at least that is what people thought. However, the Depression hit the Christoval Baptist Encampment hard. The people who attended the encampment loved it and willingly paid whatever they could toward its upkeep. But when their finances were hit by the Depression, it affected the encampment, too.

By 1932 the presiding officers realized they could not pay the bills, and the grand gathering had to stop. Gus Jones, secretary of the encampment's board of directors was quoted in the *Baptist Standard* as saying, "Due to financial reasons and as a matter of economy the board of directors voted unanimously to not hold the 1932 session at Christoval Baptist Encampment. They regret exceedingly to do this, but under circumstances in West Texas, they deem it advisable."

The tabernacle became a skating arena under new ownership. Later it housed a semi-pro basketball team. Some of the cabins and other buildings lay in the flood plain, and high water in the early 1930s washed them away.

Not all preachers had pretty blue river water available when time came for a baptism to take place. Whether he was preaching or baptizing, Millican used what facilities were available. In 1895 L. R. Millican baptized his friend Joe Evans. As Joe described the ceremony, he said, "L. R. baptized me in a water hole with mud up to my knees." It was probably the nearest water Millican could find.

As motor vehicles emerged in the 1900s, preachers switched their trusty saddle horse for a gas-guzzling "tin lizzy." Cars gave Millican a lot of problems. He was always in a hurry, the car was too light, and he often ended up in trouble. Once he turned over in a ditch, several times. On another trip, he and his car ended up at the bottom of the hole made for a new cattle guard that was unfinished. In one of his accidents, Millican was pinned under the car with the vehicle upside down. But he survived all of his car accidents. By 1926 he was traveling some 24,605

Joe Evans said that Brother Millican baptized him in a mud hole. Since there were cattle in the Davis Mountain area, this scene is similar to Millican's baptistery. Author's collection.

miles a year and complained about his terrible car expenses. Being the ripe young age of 74, he felt the Baptist Association should help with his gas bill.

What time Millican was not preaching, he was checking on his own ranch. He always had a little spread, and from 1892 to 1929, he owned a 14,000-acre ranch ten miles west of Van Horn near Sierra Blanca. It was in the proximity of his churches in the El Paso region. This ranch would have been in Hudspeth County, some 70 miles southeast of El Paso.

Hudspeth County was bordered by New Mexico to the north, the Mexican state of Chihuahua to the south, El Paso County to the west and Culberson and Jeff Davis counties to the east. Millican's ranch land would have been a combination of wide open prairies and mesa-shaped mountains.

The distance from his ranch to the rest of the state was a slight problem. If Millican checked cows near Van Horn and wanted to go to a statewide church meeting in Fort Worth, he was about 500 miles away from the gathering.

Millican and his wife had two sons, Elliott and Judson, when they lived in Hudspeth County. Judson entered Baylor University in 1900, when he was only sixteen or seventeen years old. From the ranch, Baylor was close to 600 miles away and his parents knew they would not see him very much, but Judson convinced them to let him try his wings.

Judson Millican did not forget the people he met in Hudspeth County and along the Rio Grande. This boy must have had a longing to live and work in Mexico because he got there as quickly as he could. As soon as he graduated from college, he began teaching in Chihuahua, Mexico. Not long after he began educating his pupils, Judson contracted typhoid fever and died. Many years before, the Millicans had a daughter who was bitten by a spider when she was three years old. The incident happened at a camp meeting at Lampasas. The family told about Leander Millican holding his young daughter as he knew she was dying. He asked her to sing "Come to Jesus Just Now," and she sang in her daddy's arms until her last breath trailed away.

In the next year after Judson's death, the Millicans realized that their older son, Elliott, was also very sick. Doctors identified his illness as diabetes. Mother Millican would tell him not to eat certain foods, but he was a grown man with a family. He did not always mind his mother. January 16, 1907, Elliott also died. Two weeks after losing their last son, the Millicans had a baby named Nevada Katherine.

In spite of all the suffering that Millican endured, he still helped the people around him. When cattlemen needed a spokesman in Austin, Millican was there. He gave speeches explaining the need for ranchers to share in oil benefits, schools and roads, or relief from drought. Millican spent most of his waking hours thinking of the people around him. At least, his men in the pews always knew he cared for them and shared the same needs. This attitude made him a great preacher.

Hudspeth County not only was the home of Millican's ranch but also claimed the famous Indian Hot Springs, which were located thirty-three miles west of Sierra Blanco along the Rio Grande. Apache Indians gave the bubbling waters their name because this liquid had medicinal power to heal wounds. While Millican rode this area horseback, he would have met the Babbs family.

In the early 1900s, Jewell Babbs, with her son's help, ran a health resort at the springs. She had a 22-room stone hotel at that location where people could stay and take baths. Mexican women helped her keep the hotel and the cottages surrounding it clean.

Jewell Babbs came from a ranching family and knew how to make ends meet when the going was rough. Therefore, she did not offer many frills to her clients who came for baths. They had a very rocky, rough road to negotiate to get to her place, and when they arrived, they found no clocks to control their time or telephones to connect with the outside world.

The area had its own entertainment such as the beauty to behold when the sun played with the colors of the tall Quitman Mountains nearby and coyotes howled from not very far away. This same rustic canyon was home to panthers who screamed with a chilling cry that made listeners sure they were hearing the distressed sound of a woman scared out of her wits.

While Jewell Babbs ran goats along the sparsely covered hills and provided mineral baths, Millican roamed the area to save souls and meet the ranchers. He could ride his horse at roundup time and check his cattle in Hudspeth County, or he might be clear across the state of Texas at a convention. Millican was a hard man to follow. From 1917 to 1918, he even found time to serve as county commissioner of precinct 4 of Hudspeth County.

He was also active in the statewide Baptist Conventions. One time Millican was assigned to be a member of the Committee on Credentials at the Texas Baptist Convention. He and his members had to check on the authenticity of each member attending the conference and their home church. He refused to seat one Samuel A. Hayden, and the unhappy man sued Millican and twenty-nine other Baptist leaders. This case was tried four times in the 44th District Court of Dallas, so the trial continued for eight months.

Twenty-four men were listed as defendants and only one, C. C. Slaughter, had any money. This cattleman of the Panhandle area believed in God's work as much as his dear Daddy, preacher George. Finally C. C. Slaughter paid Hayden a settlement of $7,500, and the man dropped the charges. Money seemed more important to the man than being a delegate to the Baptist Convention. This C. C. Slaughter was the son of George Slaughter who had served the Lord from the time he drove a wagon for Texas's leaders in the Texas Revolution until he hung up his spurs in the Panhandle country for good.

L. R. Millican, who was relieved to hear that Hayden dropped the charges against him, got into the middle of some unreligious activities as well. When several people in 1896 wanted El Paso to host the famous boxing match between Peter Maher, the Irish boxer, and Ruby Fitzsimmons, the current U. S. champion, Millican thought otherwise. He organized protests that took the fight away from El Paso.

Millican wanted it out of the United States because he thought it encouraged gambling. He managed to have it moved by protesting the show so much so that organizers looked elsewhere for a location. The preacher's life was threatened because some ambitious citizens of El Paso wanted the fight in their town. In some mysterious way, the Texas Rangers were notified about the El Paso bout, and they entered the town to prevent such a happening. New Mexico and Arizona wanted the bout also, but President Glover Cleveland signed a bill that Congress passed on February 7, 1896, which actually outlawed such fights in the Territories of New Mexico and Arizona. This bill passing occurred seven days before the bout was to occur.

With the law and preachers like Millican against the boxing match in El Paso, the fight promoters looked elsewhere. They thought that Juarez, Mexico, might be a good location. However, a joint conference of U. S.-Mexican officials meeting February 12, 1896, stopped that idea. About the middle of February, Judge Roy Bean decided he had the best spot for the fight near his home at Langtry, Texas.

At that time, he sent a telegram to the boxing promoters according to Jack Skiles in *Judge Roy Bean Country*. In the message, Roy Bean invited the men to have the Fitzsimmons-Maher fight in Langtry. He told them he was the law west of the Pecos and would guarantee protection. Bean fixed a boxing ring across the Rio Grande on a sand bar, and on February 20, 1896, a trainload of fans came from El Paso to Judge Roy Bean's world for a very short match. The actual bout took all of one minute and thirty-five seconds for Fitzsimmons to knock out Maher, but Millican won some satisfaction by keeping the match out of El Paso.

While Millican was trying to outwit Judge Roy Bean, another preacher was quoting scripture on the Pecos River not far from Millican. Clay Allison, sometime preacher and sometimes outlaw, once held a service in the town of Pecos, up the river quite a distance from Langtry. Allison could hit a person with words or with bullets from his gun. He was the West's version of Dr. Jekyll and Mr. Hyde.

Allison was so worried about the transgressions of the men around Pecos, Texas, that he decided to hold a worship service in the Lone Wolf Saloon. He admonished the men present to sing "Shall We Gather at the River," even though they were only a stone's throw from the Pecos River. Then with his six-shooter nearby, he commenced to preach on the marvelous story of Jonah and the whale. As he preached, he admitted the story was hard to believe because that fish would have to be as "big in the barrel as the Pecos River and have an opening in his face bigger than Phantom Lake Cave."

He asked his crowd if they believed that story to put their hands up. Only two or three responded. Then he fussed at the motley group of ranchers, stage drivers and storekeepers to have more faith. Finally, after he exhorted them to believe, he had all the hands in the air. Everybody believed that the whale swallowed Jonah. His sermon was better than his real-life actions. Allison's love for alcohol brought about his death. Totally drunk, he fell off a loaded freight wagon and was crushed by the horses.

If L. R. Millican ever met up with the likes of Clay Allison, it is not known. But Millican continued actively to preach, in spite of health problems, until he was 80 years old. At that time, the warhorse was turned out to pasture. On April 18, 1938, he went to his final resting place where no more horses would throw him, cars would flip over, or churches would be short of funds to pay him. He was home with the Lord.

Millican died in an El Paso hospital after having surgery. On the day he died, he told reporters, "I have been so busy living that I have had no time to think about how and when I shall die." He is buried on a hill overlooking the Paisano Baptist Encampment, twelve miles from Alpine.

Although Millican argued over prize fighting and ranchers' rights, another preacher loved to argue theology. Bill Robinson sent Methodists and Church of Christ members of Central Texas into a tizzy when he disagreed so strongly with their religious beliefs.

7

CIRCUIT RIDERS IN
CENTRAL TEXAS: 1850S–1900s

Peter Gravis, a Central Texas preacher, was well acquainted with "the school of hard knocks." He had a tough start in life. Gravis, born July 6, 1828, lost his mother when he was three and was soon uprooted from that home in Tennessee to come to Texas. Gravis traveled in a wagon with his dad and their most prized possessions: the old milk cow trailing behind them and the setting hens perched in their box on the wagon.

The family hardly had time to unpack before little Gravis tearfully watched his father leave their new home with his gun by his side. Peter Gravis's father had the misfortune to hit the Lone Star State just in time to join the fight for its independence. The little boy watched the lane in front of their house day after day in hopes that he would see his father coming home.

Finally, news came that the Union had defeated the South. Peter Gravis was overjoyed to see his father. He thought all would be well for them, but now the Gravis family had other problems. The Indian raids were so bad around their first home in Navasota that the Gravis family sought civilization near Houston.

While enjoying city life, Gravis learned some blacksmithing skills before he left home to seek his fortune. Finally the day came for him to say his farewells. This slight young man was not a very impressive sight as he walked away from the Gravis cabin with an ox cart containing two changes of clothes and his pockets stuffed with $1.50.

But interesting things began to happen to young Gravis. He found the Lord in a camp meeting near Bastrop and married his sweetheart, Mary Wright, in February 1853, in Williamson County. His decision to be a circuit-riding preacher for the Methodist Episcopal Church soon put Rev. Gravis into some scary situations in his new home, Blanco County. "The country was visited by hostile Indians every month, and it was necessary for me to go well armed and mounted on a good horse," he said. He had the latter but not the gun. Finally he rummaged around enough to find an old dragon pistol that he loaded with buckshot and suspended on the pommel of his saddle.

As Gravis rode the trails to turn wayward hearts toward God and the Methodist Episcopal Church, he met strong opposition from another denomination: the Campbellites. They were people who followed Alexander Campbell and his teachings of immersion in water when a person became a Christian. This Campbellite church joined the Baptists in 1813, but the two groups soon discovered that they had too many differences in theology. Each rather headstrong group went its separate way by 1830.

Alexander Campbell made one other attempt to join forces: this time his group aligned with the Christian Church. However, by the time Gravis of the Methodist Episcopal Church preached in Texas homes and tabernacles, the Campbellites had developed their own denomination. They were well represented in the same communities where Gravis graced the pulpit.

Preacher that he was, Gravis made a commotion in that area because he not only saved thirty or forty people at his altar calls but also stirred up the ire of these Campbellites. Since he was converting the very souls to Methodist beliefs that they had been trying to save, the Campbellites decided to discredit him. Gravis's opposition broadcast the news far and wide that Gravis was not feeding his family as he should. This criticism got back to his Methodist brethren, and they were mad at him for stirring up the wrath of the Campbellites. Peter Gravis was on the far side of his circuit when he heard the criticism insinuating that he was a poor provider for his family. He was determined to prove them wrong, so he brought a side of bacon home while riding through Indian territory most of the way.

The food Peter Gravis brought home to his family must have satisfied his wife. Obviously, Mrs. Gravis was not too upset about the food shortage because she soon moved the children into a real parsonage when Gravis was assigned the Llano Mission. But this location caused Gravis to have a large circuit, which included a population of 1,500 people scattered over 900 square miles. He either rode his horse or had an ox cart pulled by pony or donkey to get from one community to another. During this year of 1860, Gravis bought a Colt revolver and rented some farmland.

In the Llano area, Indians constantly raided the homesteads and nearly scared the settlers to death although the painted warriors usually wanted only the horses. Night after night the Indian calls could be heard as they added more ponies to their ramada. Eventually, Gravis lost his only steed to them, and his neighbors lost theirs as well. There was nobody who could loan the preacher a horse, so he had to walk seven miles one way to some cabins and fifteen miles to the other settlement where he preached.

One time when preacher Gravis was away from home, the Indians came to his homestead. His wife hid the children under the bed and waited in terror. However, when the Indians saw no horses around the homestead, they realized there was nothing to steal. Eventually the redskins left the Gravis cabin. But once the warriors were discovered in that area, some neighbors saddled up to give chase. They followed the warriors into Burnet County where they caught them and opened fire. The local militia retrieved some ponies including the preacher's old horse that had been missing for quite a while.

About the same time that the settlers were attacking the Indians, Gravis attended a church conference in another community. The presiding elder preached a sermon to the audience and included remarks about how destitute Gravis really was. He made reference to the fact that the preacher had nothing to ride. After the sermon was finished, an old man known as a miser said he would give the parson a horse. However, he stipulated a condition that must be met in order for the preacher to receive the animal. Gravis had to appear in person to receive his gift. The church member wanted to be sure the needy preacher got the horse rather than somebody else who just wanted a handout.

While Gravis was preaching in Central Texas, Rev. Jacob P. Sneed began extolling Christian virtues to groups of people around Waco, Texas. This community was young when he visited, and it eventually had streets laid out in 1848–1849. By 1850 the Village of Waco owned a small log cabin and allowed Sneed to preach there.

A good sermon could last three hours. In fact, this was standard length for such a preacher as Sneed. On the particular day that he preached in the cabin, his text was Proverbs 3:6, "In all they ways, acknowledge Him and He shall direct they paths." Sneed slept on a saddle blanket under a tree after the services. He awoke when some wolves started howling nearby and luckily survived their advances.

Sneed and his Methodist friends eventually decided to build a church at Second and Jackson Street in the Village of Waco. Sawmills in that area had horse-drawn equipment so that the saw blade moved as horses walked in a circle, supplying the power. After making an agreement with the mill owner, the church members saw their dream take shape. Planks made the walls and split logs made the benches for churchgoers to use.

The completed structure had a price tag of $1,000. This amount was probably thought to be very extravagant in 1850. Since everybody in Waco knew each other, the Baptists and the Presbyterians shared the new building with the Methodist owners. However they may have hotly argued theology, now that everybody needed a building, the members of the three churches had a different attitude. The three denominations used the church and met at different times.

The Methodist congregation grew in Waco, and by 1868, it started building a bigger church at Third and Franklin. This edifice cost $8,000 and had some famous people visit. During 1861, Sam Houston spoke there against secession. He wanted Texas to remain in the Union no matter what other states did. He voiced the same feelings when he spoke on the steps of the nearby courthouse.

As early as 1845, the Republic of Texas issued a charter for Baylor University, a Baptist college in Waco. The Methodists were always in competition with the Baptists, so they got very busy and started a school of their own.

The Methodist people around Waco decided to organize the Waco Female College, chartered February 11, 1860. This institution was formed with the following streets as boundaries: Webster, Jackson, Third and Second Streets. Since the college had a large auditorium, the local Methodist congregation met there for a while on the second floor before they built an equally large church for their members.

Several years later, the people of Central Texas had other thoughts than that of building churches. The Civil War affected every Texan in some way. Peter Gravis's world turned topsy-turvy when the war hit Texas in 1862. His choices were either to join the Confederacy or to leave Texas. Since he was not sympathetic to the Southern cause, he did not like either alternative. The declaration of war left the schools with no professors, forts with no soldiers and Indians running unrestrained through the settlements.

At the Texas Methodist Conference, ministers made speeches about killing the enemy as "though they were beasts of prey." Gravis was against secession, just as Sam Houston was, so the church made it hard on Gravis. Although he continued to preach and serve God, he received no financial help for his wife and four children. The Methodists leaders expected him to fight for the South.

Eventually, Peter Gravis had to move his family to Llano and with the move came an abrupt decision. He joined Capt. Mabry's Confederate troops where he was chaplain to infantry soldiers. The parson hopefully had a good horse by that time because he made trips that were terribly long compared to his circuit trips. Gravis shot to kill as he fought with his regiment in New Orleans and then at Vicksburg. During one battle, the Confederates fielded 17,000 troops to the Union's 35,000 men, but Peter Gravis now thought like a true soldier. For the first time, he believed in the cause for which the Confederates were fighting. Although he did not want the South to split from the Union, Gravis was convinced that God would give the Confederates a victory.

He felt this so strongly that he never thought about dying. The Confederate army won that battle, but as Gravis rode from one group of soldiers to another with little rest and food, he became the sick man on the litter. Finally he returned home to Texas to recuperate in 1864. Rest was short for the ailing preacher because he was appointed chaplain of a frontier army in Texas.

Another preacher, Rev. Anthony Bewley, was involved in the Civil War in a different way: Anthony grew up in the south but was against slavery. His conviction caused him to speak out in 1845 when his Methodist church decided to join the Methodist Episcopal Church. Those members who were against slavery broke away and formed the Northern Church. This was Bewley's preference, too. He had already spent many hours in the saddle since he started his preaching as a youngster in Virginia. Once he succeeded in "rightly dividing the truth" to his home church, he rode from settlement to settlement spreading God's word. After marrying Jane Winton in 1834, he moved to Missouri and continued telling people about God's love.

Eventually, Bewley decided to move westward, so he brought his family to Arkansas, only to move westward once more. Finally he established a mission sixteen miles south of Fort Worth, in 1858. He thought the slavery issue would not be as heated in Texas, but he was wrong. Whereas the northern Methodists thought Bewley preached watered-down messages about abolition, these Texans decided he was on the opposite side of the question from them; he preached too strongly against slavery. Bewley's beliefs became a real problem.

In the summer of 1860, vigilance committees spread a rumor in Texas that there was a dangerous abolitionist plot to burn towns and murder citizens. Anyone who spoke against slavery was in trouble, Bewley included. Soon after the Reverend unpacked his family's belongings in the Fort Worth area, a fire broke out in the business district of town. Other fires erupted across Texas, and Bewley was blamed for the raging flames. About the same time as the smoldering fires died down, a nearby slave, known as Ned, told his master that the northerners urged the Negroes in the area to revolt.

This remark ignited a different flame as southern sympathizers wanted to find these intruders. Bewley was considered a northern sympathizer. To make matters worse, on July 3, 1860, a letter addressed to Bewley got into the vigilantes' hands. The contents of the letter supposedly encouraged the parson to continue his work in helping to free Texas from slavery.

Bewley maintained that the letter from fellow abolitionist William H. Bailey was a forgery. Even so, it was published in many newspapers, and people believed that the parson worked with the John Brownites in Texas. They practically placed the flaming torch that burned nearby buildings in Bewley's hands. This turn of events led Bewley to depart quickly toward Kansas with part of his family. He waited eleven days in Indian Territory for the rest of his family to join him. Once his entire brood was together, Bewley hit the road once more and stopped only long enough to visit with friends in Benton County, Arkansas.

Sadly for Bewley, his attackers rode the same trail. Although Bewley whipped his teams of horses and exhorted them to run faster, the vigilantes chasing him gained ground. Run as he might, the anti-slavery preacher was caught by his assailants who called themselves a posse. Bewley was taken into custody in Cassville, Missouri. Bewley, now a prisoner, rode the long trail back to Fort Worth, bound with rope to prevent escape. He was helpless, and as he looked at his captors, he saw their eyes glowing with hatred. A few days later they returned to Cow Town with their prisoner.

On the night of September 13, 1860, the parson was turned over to a lynch mob and hanged near Fort Worth. Although Bewley's body was buried the next day in a shallow grave, it was not the parson's final destination. Three weeks later, somebody removed his bones from the grave, stripped them of any remaining flesh and placed the skeleton on top of Ephraim Daggett's storehouse. Children actually played with his bones. After this hanging, the Northern Methodists quietly left Texas, probably under the cloak of darkness.

A few years later, church members felt the struggle between Unionists and Confederates at the Episcopal Church in Austin. Rev. Charles Gillette, the pastor of St. David's Church preached to a congregation of Unionists, but he had a Confederate bishop named Alexander Gregg who closely observed his work. The bishop wrote a prayer that supported the Confederates and insisted it be used in all meetings. Gillette would dutifully pray all the words in the prayer except the part, "grant that the unnatural war which has been forced upon us, may speedily be brought to a close."

Gillette was in trouble in 1862 because the annual church convention voted that all parishes must read the prayer in full. This brought about more dissension because people began to say Gillette favored the doctrine of Lincoln while Bishop Gregg preferred the doctrine of the "gospel according to Jeff Davis." Finally, words got so hot that Gregg had to leave Texas, never to return.

While the Methodist ministers and Episcopalians fought over the Civil War, another denomination was determined to compete for Texas souls also. The Baptists were close behind the Methodists and Episcopalians as they brought the message of Jesus to a new land. As Baptists entered Texas, they were splintered into several different names. A Baptist believer might be Regular, Separate, United, General, Particular, Primitive or Freewill. Although the first church to be organized in Texas that carried the name Baptist was listed as being in Bastrop in 1834, many Baptists hitched their wagons or ox carts and headed west. This area of the state brought new challenges to the brethren that believed in submersion.

In the 1850s, the word "road" meant two deep ruts in the prairie. Most families did well to have tar-pole wagons pulled by five or six yoke of oxen. Rivers had no bridges, so travelers were often stranded for days or even weeks by flood waters raging downstream. If a circuit rider was stranded on the wrong side of the stream, his family back home had no way of knowing his predicament. As far as they knew, their family member might have met an Indian raiding party.

Preachers who traveled on a single horse rather than a wagon still had problems. One circuit rider wrote to George Baines, editor of the Baptist newspaper, and told how hard it was to get horse feed in the winter. The editor wrote him back and explained that his situation would be much better when spring rolled around, if he had a long "stake rope." This answer obviously solved his problem when spring rains brought new growth, and he could tie his horse to a long rope. However, the harsh winter months were still a problem.

Taking care of the horses or mules once they made it to the church house was another question that members had to solve. One church near Birdville in the Fort Worth area sent out a plea for the men to bring two forks and a pole to the next meeting. The church intended to build a hitching rack.

If the elements and caring for their animals was not enough of a problem, members of the church had to worry about breaking church rules. The early Baptist churches criticized their people if they sinned by drinking whiskey. Men were not the only family members who drank. Even the wife and children imbibed the spirits, sometimes called "medicine." Activities of gambling, lying or fornication brought down judgment by ministers also. Baptist churches disciplined some members during their Saturday conferences.

Revivals had a short form, the basket meetings, and the long form, the camp meetings. When groups of people lived in brushy, hilly regions where it was hard to meet very often, they had church meetings that lasted only Saturday and Sunday. Food in a basket was sufficient for the length of the sermons they would hear for two days. They did not bring tents but stayed with neighbors nearby. Quilts spread on the floor or in the wagon served as beds for the night.

Extended weeklong revivals were another matter. Many times they were held in the winter, so families brought tents for themselves or large tents were available to accommodate several families. More than one preacher might take turns to spread the gospel at 9 a.m., 2 p.m. and 7 p.m. People sat on logs, and an important rail divided the two sides of the congregation. Men and boys occupied one side, while women and girls sat on the opposite side. Many new converts found salvation at the mourners' bench, and people visited during the breaks between sermons.

In spite of attending church like civilized people, the early Christians had problems with the Indian raids. A person living in Stephenville wrote to a Waco paper about the terrible Indian raids in 1866. He said this is "zero hour" for the frontier in its relationships with the Indians. In August 1865, preacher Vernon's children capered about in their watermelon patch near Springtown one day, oblivious to any danger. Suddenly forty Indians burst out of a line of trees nearby and attacked the children. Vernon lost one son that awful day and had two children wounded.

On November 10, 1869, representatives from Pony Creek, Stephenville, Leon and Comanche met in Paluxy to organize the Brazos River Baptist Association. They had waited awhile to do this because of Indian problems, but felt that they needed to move forward with their plans. Messengers and preachers both kept loaded pistols handy during the meeting. Unknown to the churchmen, on Sunday night an Indian raiding party captured a group of horses scarcely a mile from their meeting place. News of the event reached the churchmen the next morning. Immediately they saddled their horses and followed the Indians' trail.

The warriors bothered church groups no matter where they assembled. While a revival took place at Weatherford in Parker County, some Indians, brazen enough to be unafraid, led stolen horses near the edge of town. When the Baptists heard how close the warriors were, they left the meeting, followed the Indians and retrieved some of the horses.

Another minister who passed through Central Texas about the same time as Gravis and Bewley did, was Choctaw Bill Robinson. Born in North Carolina in 1809 to Wallace and Rebecca Robinson, he spent his growing years in that state. As a young man, he courted a girlfriend named Julia. The two hit it off so well that wedding bells soon pealed for

Bill Robinson and Julia Lucinda Fulford on April 16, 1828. This young couple celebrated the arrival of several children in rapid order. In fact, their eight children were typical of the big families at that time. They spent a few years in Louisiana as Bill farmed and owned as many as 100 slaves to help him with his crops.

The Robinson family felt the hand of death strike as their beloved mother Julia died. A preacher with eight children to rear by himself could neither preach many sermons nor raise a crop. Bill hit the courting trail pretty fast. Widows or unmarried women were the parson's target. As luck would have it, he met and soon thereafter married Irena Isabella Bent November 15, 1846. The Robinsons were destined to have a really large family as Irena had six children with her new husband. Two years after this wedding, Bill and Irena moved to Texas in 1848. As they made this trip, all but two or three of their slaves stayed in Louisiana.

Not until Bill hit Texas did he become an ordained Baptist minister. From his location in Bellview, Bill rode his circuits with great enthusiasm as evidenced in the fact that he pastored or helped organize twenty churches.

He stood behind a pew to deliver his first sermon at Stephenville September 17, 1855. Up to that time Central Texas had few "words of the gospel" floating around the hills. Robinson preached the first sermons ever heard in Comanche by many of its citizens, as well as churchgoers from Brown County. He circulated around the oak-covered hills as he started churches at Dublin, Robinson Springs, Holly Springs, Antioch, Willow Springs, Paluxy, Green Creek, Noland's River, Cross Timbers, Harmony, Baggett Creek, Board Creek, Sipe Springs, Pony Creek, Pleasant Hill, Shiloh and Camp Colorado.

Bill and his wife Irena had fourteen children by 1850, counting his first and second families. However, the life of a circuit rider was not that of a good father. Bill was gone from home a lot of the time, so his children hardly knew him. They saw him as that man who came home now and then, often wearing a dusty black coat from miles of travel.

Someone else had to step in and help milk the cows and plow the fields. The older son, Williamson Milburn, did manage the farm and livestock while his father was preaching. If Robinson's churches were nearby, he could leave on Friday night and preach a Saturday sermon and another on Sunday before coming home.

Reverend William "Choctaw Bill" Robinson was a Baptist minister who enjoyed arguing theology with other denominations. Courtesy of Patsy Mears, great-granddaughter of Bill Robinson.

The church facilities that Robinson used were rather primitive. His church members sat on oak logs split down the middle. The flat side faced upward for a seat and pegs placed in the holes on the curved side kept the benches upright. These seats had no backs on them, much to the chagrin of people who sat on these pews as they listened to Bill exhort the Bible passages for several hours.

Bill Robinson was as stalwart in his Baptist beliefs as Peter Gravis was about his Methodist ones. Bill preached the "landmarkism viewpoint," which says that all other denominations except his Baptist belief were false. This concept brought some interesting confrontations among backwoods Methodists and Campbellite believers.

But he argued the Bible only part of his time. Sometimes he held weddings to get a young couple hitched like the one planned in the winter of 1859. The location for this event was at a home between Robinson Peak in Coleman County and Buffalo Gap in Taylor County. That mountain was named for the preacher Robinson. Just before the ceremony, Indians sounded their war whoop and rode up to the cabin. Of all the terrible things that could happen, this raid was the worst because they captured the bride-to-be, dressed in her prettiest finery. A snowstorm developed after the raid and made it even more difficult for Robinson and several other men to track the warriors. In these freezing conditions, the determined wedding guests urged their horses forward. Finally, they located the Indian camp and recaptured the girl. As soon as she returned to the cabin, the wedding went off without another hitch.

Other circuit riders preached in areas not too far from Coleman. The San Saba River area had one preacher who appeared now and then at the cabin doors. When this particular parson rode up to a cowman's home near Pecan Crossing, he told the cowboy he would like to preach to the neighbors around, if the man would help him spread the word. The rancher looked at him very seriously and asked, "I want to know straight out whether you are a cowman's preacher or a sheepman's preacher?"

The parson looked around to see if he could see a sheep or smell one. When neither happened, he said, "I'm a cowman's preacher." The cowboy had him stay overnight with him both Friday and Saturday nights. The preacher realized that the cattleman rustled up a good crowd for Sunday morning as he surveyed the people sitting under the brush arbor at Pecan Crossing on the San Saba River.

The preacher did not see his host, the cowboy, but he started the service without him. After his introduction, he chose his text as the twenty-third Psalm. Just as he started to speak, he saw his friend walk toward a pew. But when the preacher recited, "The Lord is my Shepherd," he noticed the cowboy turn and walk away.

After the sermon was finished, the preacher rode back to the house where he had stayed the last two nights. There on the porch sat his friend the cowboy. He could not help but ask the cattleman why he left the service so quickly. The man looked at him menacingly and said, "I rounded up that crowd of people because you said you were a cowman's preacher. When you started preaching, the first words I heard you say were, 'The Lord is my shepherd.' The next time you want to preach in this country, you can go somewhere else."

Probably no Texas preacher could out perform Bill Robinson who preached his viewpoints with a lot of gusto. One time he said, "I'm going to run the devil into a hollow log and cut his tail off and punch out the pith and give the hollow tail to some of my good Methodist friends to use as a squirt gun to sprinkle their babies."

Bill Robinson not only had words for the Methodists but also for the Campbellites. In one of his sermons, he conducted court with Alexander Campbell on trial. He brought witnesses like Peter, Paul and John to testify against Campbell. Some people who attended Robinson's service believed in the teachings of Alexander Campbell. Robinson angered the churchgoers when he talked against their views, so they arose to leave the service. Robinson said to them, "That's it. Got your little jug full and afraid you'll pop if you stay. Just go ahead."

In 1861, Robinson moved his family to a place near Camp Colorado, which was in Coleman County. In 1856, U. S. soldiers built the first Camp Colorado, which was located on the Mukewater River. After months of playing carpenter instead of soldier, the troopers saw their fort completed. However, during the next year, seven soldiers came down with malaria, and the drought reduced the Mukewater River to a trickle. Soldiers moved their fort's location to a place on the Jim Ned River, twenty miles north. It was this second location where Robinson preached.

Robinson may have lived in one of the fort buildings or in a nearby cabin. Both were made of picket. The buildings at that time were not fancy accommodations, for there were no trees large enough to make true log cabins. To make a picket wall, soldiers stood many vertically trimmed logs side by side in a ditch, covered their lower ends with dirt and daubed mud between the logs to keep the cold wind out.

When Robinson began to preach in Coleman County, the Methodists decided that Gravis should also preach there when he was not filling the pulpit at Comanche or Dublin. Not long after he got to Camp Colorado, Gravis heard that Bill Robinson had argued with two local Methodist preachers, and they could not take the harassment.

The Methodists decided to fight back. Gravis was informed that he would have to stand up to the noisy Bill Robinson. Being a sandy-haired Irishman, Gravis said, "I've been doing that for two long years and am well experienced. I have eaten slippery elm bark for supper and breakfast and slept under the cannon's roar, but let's have peace."

Nothing seemed to stop Robinson. When his Baptist flock would worship with Gravis's Methodists, Robinson would call them "tender-toed

During the 1800s, many circuit riders preached under tabernacles like this wooden one at Baggett, Texas, in Comanche County. Author's collection.

coyotes." The name-calling and difference of opinion on theology got so bad between the Baptists and the Methodists that the Leon Baptist Church offered 500 head of cattle for scriptural proof of the Methodist doctrine preached by Gravis: they were concerned about infant baptism. Gravis accepted the challenge with delight. Some accounts of this debate say that Gravis held forth for six days, and other accounts say that his boss in the Methodist Church, Elder J. M. Johnson, replaced him. Which man preached is uncertain, but peace and harmony were restored after this marathon discussion.

Bill Robinson continued to preach extended sermons, sometimes as long as four hours, but a lot of people did not like the lengthy messages. He not only preached to soldiers at Camp Colorado but also sold them beef. Robinson would also preach to an Indian, if he had the chance.

There was a Ranger Camp nearby on Hord's Creek where the Tonkawa Indians found refuge. They were an Indian band, small in numbers because they had been severely beaten by larger tribes. Robinson preached to the Indians, and some accepted Christ as their savior and were baptized. As long as Robinson was around the camp, the Indians stayed nearby. However, the soldiers in the camp did not like this, so they devised a way to get rid of the warriors. They told them that being baptized caused their evil deeds to wash off into the creek, and these deeds washing along in the river would make the Indian children sick. The Tonkawas moved away and refused to listen to any more preaching.

One day Baptist Robinson watered his horse at a Methodist widow's trough. Out of the corner of his eye, Robinson noticed the woman was watching him, so he sprinkled water on his horse to make fun of the Methodist belief in sprinkling. As he stood by the trough, he talked to her about the mistake that Methodists made when they sprinkled their converts instead of baptizing them. He also mentioned the first known baptism in the New Testament when he said, "How long was the gourd handle John the Baptist used to sprinkle Jesus?"

She angrily replied, "Just as long as the handle of that branding iron you used to brand my bull yearling." For once, Robinson had no reply. He got on his horse and rode away quite speechless.

Besides selling beef to Camp Colorado, Robinson also sold it to the troops at Fort Belknap during the Civil War. He always rode his special mule when he was alone checking his cattle or riding to a church to preach. He swore that the mule was so smart that it would let him know if an Indian was nearby.

Preacher Robinson realized there were quite a few Baptists along the Brazos River, so he and some other pastors organized the Brazos River Baptist Association October 2, 1858. During that meeting at the Providence Church in Parker County, families present envisioned a private school for their children. After much discussing, those representatives of the twelve churches organized the Brazos Institute and raised $7.20 toward its financing. The school idea continued to simmer for another year as the finance committee of George W. Slaughter, John Hittson and Bill Robinson raised $1,500 toward the building fund. With the collected money, they built a stone building, and its doors opened in 1861 to seventy pupils taught by three teachers.

The school idea, off to a good start, had a short life. By 1861, the doors of the Brazos Institute closed. Some people said the closing came about because of a faulty building, but others thought the chaos of the imminent Civil War brought about its demise.

George Slaughter must have later teamed up with a man named Hartman to open another school because a student named Ephraim Heath was valedictorian of Hartman & Slaughter Academy. This young man ran a store in Rockwell for four years where he was elected county judge in 1882. The temperance movement was in full swing at this time and Ephraim, a delegate to the Temperance Convention of 1890, took part in the New York trip.

When judges and lawyers fought against liquor, the breweries had a horrible time. But a few men who stood up for prohibition were neither judges nor lawyers. Men like Richard M. Gano pounded the pulpit to hammer home prohibition ideas and made a speaking tour during the 1887 Prohibition Campaign. Parson Gano had some interesting experiences even before he dabbled in prohibition.

Richard Gano graduated from the Louisville Medical University in Virginia in the mid-1800s. He and his wife Martha lived in Kentucky and Louisiana before arriving in Texas. They settled in Grapevine Prairie where he farmed, ranched and practiced medicine. In 1858 Richard Gano helped his neighbors chase a Comanche raiding party in Parker and Wise counties. This activity set the stage for his next endeavor. Richard Gano served under John Hunt Morgan during the Civil War. His forces fought Union soldiers at Cabin Creek in Indian Territory where Richard felt the blast of enemy fire and the pain of his wound. During this maneuver, the Confederates captured an enemy supply train worth two million dollars. Richard Gano received the title of brigadier general on March 17, 1865.

Gen. Gano traded titles after the war, for he became a minister for the Disciples of Christ. He moved his family to Dallas County by 1870 where his father also carried the title of "minister." Not only was Gano a doctor, general, and minister, he also ranched. As two of his sons grew to manhood, Richard Gano opened a real estate business with them.

What time he had left over from all his other jobs, Gano led in Bible study. He was not alone as he preached against the evils of alcohol. A group of citizens and preachers started the Anti-Saloon League to fight the wicked spirits in a bottle. Since the group wanted to get their message out to the people, they organized programs. Crowds of families listened to fiery speakers declare the evil of drink. Such a gathering usually ended in the enjoyment of a picnic, but the Anti-Saloon

League swayed people to their way of thinking. Prohibition leaders pushed the legislature to ban alcohol consumption, and that law took effect in 1907–1908.

Prohibition hit Texas breweries hard. In fact, the San Antonio Brewery Association was the only one that survived in that town. Hard-working owner Emma Koehler kept it afloat during the rough times by producing soft drinks and running a creamery business. At one time, she directed the largest brewery in the state, which made 10,000 barrels per year. Now that prohibition was in effect, Emma's beer business came to a grinding halt.

Most preachers wished they could have put Emma out of business for good, but she survived until it was legal to sell alcohol once more. When word sounded across the country that prohibition ended September 15, 1933, Emma flew into action. Within fifteen minutes of the hour it was proclaimed, Emma had one hundred trucks and twenty-five boxcars loaded with Pearl beer, so they could roll out of her gates.

Whether prohibition succeeded or not, Bill Robinson never left the rolling hills of Central Texas. He pastored four churches during 1859. In Erath County he preached, but he also ranched and was postmaster at Paluxy. A few years later he moved again to start a different business. Robinson built a gristmill and sawmill in Hazel Dell, a small community in southeastern Comanche County. The building of the sawmill on Mill Branch in 1869 was the reason the community developed. However, Robinson complained often about how violent a community it was. Hazel Dell had a saloon, a ten-pin alley and a store. Lumber from the mill helped build the little town. By 1871 a person could receive mail in the Hazel Dell post office.

Although the community had a nondenominational church, Bill Robinson sometimes preached across the street from the businesses under a large oak tree. He laid his guns in the forks of the tree and ripped into his sermons.

On some occasions, he had the words rolling so well that he preached for four hours. According to legend, some Choctaw Indians came to listen to him preach while Bill let loose with one of his long discourses. The Indians left after a while and were heard to say, "White man lie. Him talk too long." From that event, the preacher became known as "Choctaw Bill," and the tree was named "Choctaw Robinson Oak."

This Robinson Oak marker rests under a spreading oak tree near the site of the village named Hazel Dell. Choctaw Bill Robinson helped to develop Hazel Dell and preached near this location. Author's collection.

This preacher numbered himself as one of the first ten citizens who came to Hazel Dell, and he admitted that the environment attracted some rough characters. Ranchers came to buy their supplies in Hazel Dell, but drifters and outlaws visited the community too. In the county records, the story of murders, hangings and cattle rustling indicated that the town was not filled with all saintly people. Choctaw Bill often lamented that he was the only one of the original ten citizens who survived living in Hazel Dell. The others succumbed to violent deaths.

Choctaw Bill and Peter Gravis crossed trails with other interesting ministers in Central Texas. Hugh Childress, who was a great speaker as well as a good Indian fighter and bear hunter, also preached among the oak trees and sand of Comanche County. One tale told about the rugged man indicated that he once killed a bear on Sunday. Whether this occurred before or after he preached is uncertain.

Bill Robinson was quite wealthy when he arrived in Texas, but as an eighty-year-old man, he was dirt poor. As an elderly man he wrote to the State Baptist paper, "I have preached on the Texas frontier from the

Red River to the Rio Grande. Now I am old and feeble with no finances and no home. Help me what you can."

Robinson's adversary, Peter Gravis, began to analyze his life in the saddle also. By 1866 the Northwest Texas Conference of Methodists grew to a total membership of 4,500. Peter Gravis explained in his book, *Twenty-five Years on the Outside Row* why the Methodist Church always gave him the difficult circuit assignments. He said it was because, "I was light for running and small to shoot at by the Indians, so the Bishop gave me the outside row." His Stephenville Circuit was huge, 180 miles around it to be exact. Gravis evaded Indians successfully, but he and his horse ended up in a flooded river on one trip. After quite a time of floundering around, they climbed out onto the bank.

Baptist preacher George Slaughter and Methodist Peter Gravis were friends while living near each other. George left East Texas, heading west, and had a stopover in Comanche. These two circuit riders took turns preaching at revivals in Central Texas. The Indians were still a very real threat, so they both spoke many a time with two revolvers stuck in their pants or a scabbard and their rifle within arm's length. The people in the pew had their guns handy also.

After many years toiling for the Lord, Peter Gravis began to receive positions in the church leadership. He was appointed Presiding Elder of the Comanche Methodist District in 1874. As he moved into this community, he thought the position would be a promotion. Instead, he got much closer to some outlaws than he wanted to be. The rogues were none other than the Hardin brothers.

Joe and his little brother John Wesley Hardin were the sons of a God-fearing Methodist circuit rider, James G. Hardin. The boys' early years were spent near Bonham where their parents lived, and their father preached. After a while, the circuit rider moved his family to Moscow in Polk County and then to Sumpter in Trinidad County. Hardin taught school and eventually opened an academy, which both boys attended. By 1861, Hardin had studied for the bar well enough to pass his exams. Now their father was a preacher, teacher and a lawyer.

Although life looked promising for preacher Hardin, his teenage son John grew restless at home and left for greener pastures. He found himself in arguments frequently and shot several men to death while he was just a teenager. However, his brother Joe finished school and became a

Reverend James Hardin, father of outlaw John Wesley Hardin, was a school teacher as well as a lawyer. Courtesy of Walter Dixon. James Hardin was Walter Dixon's great-uncle-in-law.

lawyer. In 1872 Joe Hardin moved to Comanche and prepared to live the good life. However, in two short years the lawyer found himself on the wrong side of the law.

The preacher's other son, John Wesley Hardin, killed Brown County Deputy Sheriff Charlie Webb in a Comanche saloon in 1874. While John successfully skipped out of the reach of lawmen, they were able to capture his brother Joe and cousins, the Dixon brothers.

Joe Hardin and the Dixon brothers became inmates of the two-storied, rock Comanche jail. Lawmen felt that a jailbreak might be attempted. Strangers, armed to the teeth, moved about town, so the jail was well guarded. One night shortly after the guards changed in the jailhouse, ten or twelve men rode up to the jail quietly. The jailer, standing outside the rock building, did not pay much attention to them ambling across the square. But when the lead horseman rode straight up to the jailer and jabbed a double-barreled shotgun in his face, he knew the prisoners were in trouble. Several of the riders quickly relieved the lawmen of their guns while other vigilantes gagged the prisoners and moved them outside where horses awaited them. Some Texas Rangers, as well as the deputies that just went off duty, slept through the ordeal as they slumbered on the second floor of the jail.

A fourth prisoner, Jim Anderson, was questioned by the vigilantes and later turned loose. He was urged to leave town and never return. The hanging of the three prisoners took place, by most accounts, two or three miles southwest of Comanche. Since people believed the vigilantes came from Brown and Coleman counties; this location would mark the return path the men probably took.

When neighbors found the dead men, the Dixon brothers were chained together and hanged from the same tree; Joe Hardin, the young lawyer with a preacher for a dad, dangled from another tree close by. A friend, Mart Fleming, cut the boys down and took their dead bodies to Hardin's house. Parson Peter Gravis preached the funeral for these men although he was in a dangerous position. A mob threatened him while he preached, and some accounts say the Texas Rangers were called in to help keep the peace while he quoted scripture over the dead men.

After the funeral, Hardin sent word to his wayward son, John Wesley. He told him not to surrender. He did not want to see his second son swing from a rope. Hardin thought if John ever came back to Comanche, the whole family might be wiped out, so he told him to leave that area around home for good. Eventually, lawmen or vigilante groups in retaliation for Deputy Sheriff Webb's death killed eight of the Hardin family members.

Somehow the citizens of Comanche County survived, but the burial site of the three gunmen, Joe and the Dixon brothers, was always a point in question. Many years later the Hardin property came into the possession of William Barnes, a Comanche hardware merchant. Mrs. Barnes did not want to be "living with the ghosts of the Hardin gang," so her husband hired two men to exhume the remains of the hanged victims. The diggers found some boot heels, buttons, belt buckles and a few larger bones. These remains were placed in a wooden dry goods box and buried in the Oakwood Cemetery.

Since Hardin lost one son to the rope, he tried to help his other son John Wesley escape the lawmen who were usually a short distance behind him. In 1871, the posse chased John Hardin while he rode a horse belonging to the man he had killed, Jim Smolly. When the fugitive made it to his father's house, his Dad knew John Wesley was in trouble, so he exchanged horses with John and watched his hunted child disappear down the road. Supposedly, some lawmen caught young Hardin that night as he slumbered near his campfire. While captured, John waited until the following night in camp and watched his captors doze off, one by one. He shot them and headed for home once more.

When John Wesley told his father that three men arrested him while he was asleep, his Dad said, "Son, never tell this to a mortal man. I don't believe you, but go to Mexico, and go at once. I will go part of the way with you." The two Hardin men made it through the countryside unnoticed, and Hardin urged his son to continue on the trail to Mexico. The two men rode in opposite directions. In a few days, John changed his mind about going to Mexico when he got the chance to drive some cattle to Kansas.

Eventually, John killed so many men that he took his wife and children with him and tried to shake the law by living in Florida. The Texas Rangers did not give up so easily, and they tracked him through the southern states. In 1888, the Rangers captured him in Pensacola, Florida. Hardin returned with them to Comanche where he was tried and sentenced to twenty-five years in prison.

Although he never seemed to mention his Christian upbringing when he was gunning down innocent men, John had time to reflect on his life as he walked back and forth in his small cell. He taught Sunday School class at the penitentiary, and some of the inmates said he did a pretty good job. He even wore the title of Sunday School Superintendent and studied law while incarcerated.

John Hardin's pardon came in March 16, 1894, and he was admitted to the bar. He practiced law in El Paso but could not stay out of trouble. Constable John Selman killed John Wesley Hardin August 19, 1895, in El Paso. Preacher Hardin's life was deeply scarred by his son's life as an

John Wesley Hardin, the outlaw and lawyer, was the son of Reverend James Hardin. Courtesy of Walter Dixon.

outlaw. Historian Walter Dixon wrote to the author, "I feel that he (Rev. Hardin) died of a broken heart."

While the John Wesley Hardin story floated about Comanche, the 1880s saw some violent killings in San Saba County, just 40 miles south of Comanche. The two incidents are connected by the fact that preachers were involved in both cases. Lawlessness was rampant as shootings took place around the San Saba countryside. Some farmers and ranchers had the mob suddenly appear on their land and run them off. A few poor souls actually disappeared for good when the mob showed up at their houses.

Hartal Langford Blackwell in *Mills County—The Way It Was* explained that the San Saba Mob started at the Williams Ranch community in 1869, and a preacher was one of the leaders. Blackwell says the original mob started there as they decided to wipe out the cattle rustlers in the area. For more than twenty-five years, this group of self-proclaimed vigilantes frightened people in Brown and Mills counties. Eventually the gang crossed the Colorado River into San Saba County and continued to shoot, hang and drag people to death.

Finally a second group of men, the anti-mob, decided to take the law in their hands. Lead began to fly. Some people thought that the two opposing gangs represented the German cattlemen fighting the American ranchers. The situation, filled with violence, escalated until both sides included outlaws as well as good men.

Since the battling groups kept their guns smoking, in 1896 Gov. C. A. Culberson called in the Texas Rangers to stop the war. Ranger W. J. L. Sullivan remembered his orders stipulated he was to stop the mob violence that had been ruling that area. He took with him Dud Barker, Edgar T. Neal and Allen Maddox.

Sheriff Hudson of San Saba saw to it that the rangers had a wagon and mules to haul their provisions to a camp they made at Hannah's Crossing on the Colorado River. As the lawmen met men on both sides of the argument, they sensed anger and hatred directed toward their presence. Sullivan said that all four of the Rangers made a pact to die trying to bring order to this area.

The first thing the lawmen did was locate the mob's hideout and gather evidence. By this time, nearly everybody knew that the mob had a rendezvous point at Buzzard's Waterhole near Regency, in northern San Saba County.

While the Texas Rangers investigated the warring factions, two members of the mob, Matt Ford and Tobe Bridge, had charges brought against them for killing a man named Turner, a member of the anti-mob group. The trial was held in Austin. Govenor Hogg, Judge James Robertson and Judge Pendexter spoke in behalf of the two mob members. Judge Albert Burleson and W. C. Linden prosecuted the case, which involved 369 witnesses. When all the testimony ceased in the courtroom, the jury acquitted the two men.

Since a preacher was accused of starting the mob in the first place, church members stood on different sides of the feud. Into this situation rode circuit riders proclaiming mankind's choice of God's love or hell's fiery brimstone. Some elders of the church were concerned about the frequent barrage of pistol shots that rang out among the pecan trees of that area.

Church members sought a solution to the big problem. They wanted a preacher who could tell right from wrong. Baptist Church members in the San Saba Association voiced concern that they needed ministers who were educated and knew how to present their biblical knowledge to church members better than the men currently available to grace the pulpit. In 1882 this organization voted to help pay college expenses for a promising young preacher. After collecting money for the new project, the San Saba Association went on record in 1884 as saying they had accumulated $123.50 for James Elder, a student at Baylor College. When the Association actually met for their annual conference, they collected an extra $108 for his expenses. The educating of new ministers, however, did not directly affect the ongoing problems of the San Saba Mob.

Finally, the vigilantes of the town chased the preacher who had started all the trouble out of the country, and the four Rangers met the mob at the San Saba Courthouse Square. The Texas Rangers, led by Edgar T. Neal, were grossly outnumbered, and one mob member asked the lawmen to leave. Bystanders thought that would be the sensible thing to do since four men did not stack up very well against twenty or more. But Ranger Dudley S. Barker shot the spokesperson dead. While he had the mob's attention, he told them to leave town in two minutes or go to jail.

Surprisingly, the mob dispersed and never bothered people again. Names of the mob and the preacher were mentioned only in whispers, so most of their identities are still unknown.

Most citizens of Central Texas knew for years that the San Saba area was a rough place to be. Ross Phares in his book, *Bible in Pocket, Gun in Hand,* said, "The territory was rough, churches were few and far between and a Bible was scarce." When circuit riders agreed to preach in that countryside, they received $25 to buy a pistol and $125 to purchase a horse.

Even though mobs and vigilantes disappeared, Baptist churches in the frontier of Texas fought other battles. Preachers felt they needed to come down hard on sins such as drinking, smoking and snuff-dipping. Women felt that a little dip of snuff between their lip and lower front teeth was just the thing. Preachers thought differently. An article in the *Texas Baptist Herald* as early as September 4, 1867, said, "I despise above all things to see ladies dipping. If they are pretty, it spoils their beauty, and if they are homely, it makes them still more so."

When the parsons raised their voices against the sin of dipping, one silver-haired woman with her hair twisted tightly in a bun said, "Let's change preachers." From the pulpit, tough battles were fought against sins in general and strong drink and tobacco in particular, but the human spirit of the sinner often prevailed.

If preachers around San Saba thought that a minister's life was tough, they only needed to talk to a fort chaplain to discover just how hard a preacher's life could be.

8

TEXAS FORT CHAPLAINS:
1852–1900s

As U. S. soldiers poured into Texas during the 1800s, blistering heat and isolated forts tried the soul of every recruit in blue. Godly parsons, chaplains by name, were needed at each fort to soothe the tempers and lift the spiritual side of these exhausted soldiers. However, life at the forts was not a garden party for the recruits or the parsons. Coupled with the heat was a shortage of drinking water at posts such as Camp Colorado in present-day Coleman County. Dried riverbeds forced this garrison to seek a new location where the water supply was better. Many troopers thought they signed on to be soldiers riding carefree over the plains. Instead, they found themselves sweating in hard labor to build a barracks or mend a leaky roof.

During the early years of the chaplaincy, 1838–1861, almost any warm-blooded body could draw chaplain's pay. The chief qualification required for a man of the cloth was to show up for payday. Some hard-working lieutenants thought that army chaplains had life a mite too easy when preachers sported the title of "captain in the cavalry."

Occasionally, fort commanders looked for other men who could double as a chaplain and a soldier. In one unit, a retired cook was appointed to perform the religious services for the regiment. Finally, a congressional act passed in 1838 stated that chaplains were to act also as schoolmasters at the forts. This legislation leveled the playing field a little. Now chaplain candidates in the military had to be able to read and write as well as preach.

During the Mexican War of 1846, some Mexicans noticed that all chaplains in the United States Army were white men. When the Spanish soldiers saw no Mexican padres among the U. S. soldiers, they thought that the war was a religious one, maybe a Holy War where the Protestants fought against the Catholics. While this fact made the Spanish soldiers angry, they also thought of a way that they might retaliate.

The Mexicans stimulated desertion of U. S. troops by offering them 320 acres of land, if they were enlisted men. For deserters who were officers, the Mexicans would raise the ante a little by promising them more acreage depending on their rank. To nobody's surprise, a few U. S. soldiers traded their allegiance and became owners of Mexican ranches.

However, most of the soldiers stayed in the saddle and served the U. S. government. These soldiers in blue scattered across the broad frontier with two main objectives. They intended to fight the Indian tribes until they were subdued and man extensive coastal fortifications to protect the nation's ports. In 1856 about 25 percent of the entire federal troops were based in Texas because settlers needed their help.

Men of God rode side by side with these troops as they fought Indians. Once the soldiers returned to the fort, chaplains prepared their sermons and took care of the spiritual needs of the troops, as well as the needs of the soldiers' wives and children. Although the U. S. Army included 27,000 men after the Civil War, only thirty post chaplains were available to serve this entire army scattered from New York to California.

As early as 1851, Texas forts included ones named Inge, Lincoln, Martin Scott, Croghan, Gates, Graham and Worth. Gen. Persifor Smith oversaw construction of several more Texas forts during the 1850s. He rode his horse across the prairies and hills to examine construction at Forts Ewell, Merrill, Clark, Terrrett, Mason, McKavett, Chadbourne, Phantom Hill, Belknap and Duncan. At least sixteen more forts were built during the 1860s and 1870s. At one point, Texas had about thirty forts. They could have used the thirty U. S. chaplains just in Texas alone so each fort had a chaplain, but that did not happen.

Instead, the few preachers who took the oath to minister to soldiers in Texas taught the Bible and appeared to be all the same color. White ministers served exclusively as chaplains prior to 1884. However, black soldiers served in the army dating back to the Civil War times. Finally in 1884, Henry V. Plummer broke the color barrier and wore the title of chaplain of the 9th Cavalry Regiment. By 1898 all of the black regiments had black chaplains.

Black Buffalo Soldiers in 1890. Many such troopers were stationed at Texas forts. Courtesy of the San Angelo Standard Times, *San Angelo, Texas.*

Allen Allensworth, a Negro preacher, served in the U. S. Army with distinction. He preached to the 24th Infantry from 1886 to 1906. This young man, born a slave in 1842, spent the first years of his life in Kentucky. He escaped his homeland and served as a soldier in blue. Before hostilities ceased, he fought in the Union Army as well as the Navy during the Civil War. Years later, Allensworth served with the black troops who were often sent to Texas and other southwestern states. When he retired from his chaplaincy in 1906, he had reached the rank of lieutenant colonel, the highest-ranking black in the United States military at that time.

When chaplains like Allensworth worked with young black soldiers, they were confronted with several challenges. In the 1860s, many of these young men came straight from the slave cabins on southern plantations. With that upbringing, most of the young privates could not read nor had they ever managed for themselves. They soon realized, however, that the green fields of the South did not resemble this wild, dry area called Texas very much.

On July 28, 1866, the United States Army recognized the formation of two regiments of Negro cavalry and four of infantry. These soldiers guarded the mail, and escorted stagecoaches, cattle drives and railroad construction gangs.

The first few times that the Negro soldiers fought the Indians, the warriors could not believe their eyes. They were amazed to see men with curly hair like the buffalo. These Comanche and Kiowa braves found the Negro soldiers formidable enemies and respected the black soldiers' determination to fight. Soon they gave the black soldiers a name of respect; they called them "Buffalo Soldiers."

While the soldiers of all backgrounds found the military challenging, the chaplains did also. Both white and black preachers discovered that entrance to this job was much more demanding after the Civil War than before. When a preacher decided he wanted to be a chaplain, he faced a stiff set of requirements to be accepted by the army. An applicant had to be a regularly ordained minister and be recommended by some authorized ecclesiastical body or five accredited ministers from his denomination. Such a candidate also had to provide testimonials of his present good standing.

Some people might think that chaplains at a fort only preached and ministered at the bedside of the sick. However, this job description failed to tell the whole story. Chaplains held public religious services on post at least once each Sunday and closed with a short sermon "suited to soldiers." Chaplains also preached funeral services and ministered to the sick.

The parson's day job included teaching children living at the fort as well as enlisted men. Chaplains also helped Buffalo Soldiers and many white men learn to read and write. Often, the parson held the titles of doctor, post treasurer, librarian and gardener. Chaplains needed more than twenty-four-hour days to complete their work.

Until 1884, a person could usually identify a chaplain on the fort grounds easily by searching for the only man wearing black. The government allowed him to wear a shepherd's crook of frosted silver on a shoulder strap of black velvet. Years later the new orders proclaimed chaplains should wear the uniform called "undress for officers" but should not wear the full dress uniform of staff officers.

Monthly the chaplain sent a report to the Adjutant General's office describing the "moral condition" of his regiment or post. They listed any marriages, baptisms or other services they performed in the line of duty. A little insight into their daily lives unfolds in the monthly reports that the post chaplain submitted to the Adjutant General of the Army in Washington, D.C.

Rev. Tobias H. Michell, D.D., Protestant Episcopal Church, joined the men in service at Fort Chadbourne from a leave of absence on December 24, 1856. At that time, his titles included that of chaplain as well as schoolmaster, but his titles increased as he stayed around those cedar hills and red dirt of future Coke County. Fort Chadbourne, a fort built in 1852 on Oak Creek eleven miles northeast of present-day Bronte, Texas, protected settlers from the Comanches and Kiowas who raided in that region. Mail routes such as the Butterfield passed through this fort also.

The Indians managed to come inside Fort Chadbourne a year before Michell appeared. At that time, the warriors captured two mail carriers and burned them at the stake. Another incident happened close to the fort where Indians murdered a mail carrier between Fort Chadbourne and Fort McKavett. Troopers searched those cedar-covered hills trying to find the Indians, so the guilty warriors knew they were in deep trouble.

Months before the killings, the Indians appeared so friendly that soldiers occasionally noticed them camped near the fort. Troopers often invited the warriors to come inside. Now that the soldiers hated the murderers, they kept a vigil for the Indians. Soon the Indians tried to pull a trick. The warriors came to the fort to plead their innocence of wrongly killing any white soldiers.

The Indians' appearance at Fort Chadbourne might have worked except one Indian dropped his blanket. He exposed a rifle that belonged to one of the murdered men. The gun carried the dead mail carrier's name engraved on the stock. Another one of the Indian visitors rolled a cigarette from a piece of paper. When it fell to the floor, a soldier recognized it as a piece of a letter sent on the ill-fated trip when the carrier died.

The angry soldiers opened fire on the Indians at point-blank range and killed the visiting warriors inside the fort. Into this situation came a man of God, Michell, proclaiming that all Christians should love their enemies. This message was hard for soldiers to accept when their murdered friends lost their lives to these painted warriors.

On June 17, 1857, the Fort Chadbourne Quartermaster's report included Tobias H. Michell as on staff. He served as teacher, preacher and physician, but from time to time he took extended leaves of absence. On

June 19 of that year, he left the post for four months. No explanation was given as to his location while on leave.

In February 1858, the roster included Tobias H. Michell as medical doctor and post chaplain. Chaplains seemed to inherit the title of "medical doctor" whether they went to medical school or not. By April and May 1858, Tobias H. Michell had the initials "M. D." after his name. He also inherited the title of civilian employee associated with the Quartermaster Department. In this capacity he guided the troops and received $40 a month. Second Lt. C. W. Thomas, 1st Infantry signed as Post Commander of Fort Chadbourne at this time.

On June 30, 1858, the Quartermaster Report mentioned the condition of quarters occupied by Chaplain Michell and Lt. Phillips. This building, measuring 15 by 37 feet, had walls dividing it into three rooms. The report says their housing consisted of "three rooms of 20, 18, and 13 feet." Exactly how it partitioned into rooms is unclear. The report said that the oak timber in the room showed spots of decay.

The mention of rotten timbers in the buildings brought up a question: how could this happen in a building not very old? This fort, erected in 1852, did not have permanent buildings at once. For several years, soldiers lived in drafty tents. Finally stonecutters from San Antonio shaped rocks from nearby quarries to build the fort. Eventually, soldiers moved into stone barracks buildings, but when Dr. Michell lived at Fort Chadbourne, he lived in barracks made of timber. The commanding officer filed a report about the decay and attributed it to the type of wood used, post oak.

Dr. Michell rejoined the Post January 12, 1859. By the spring of 1860, Fort Chadbourne needed another medical doctor because Dr. Smith intended to leave the fort. He hoped to receive a promotion to another location, but he had to leave the fort first to take an exam by the Army Medical Board. Dr. Charles H. Smith recommended Dr. Michell to take over his medical duties at Fort Chadbourne when he wrote, "Dr. T. H. Michell—well known to the Department as having at a previous time officiated most satisfactorily as medical officer both here and at Camp Verde." Dr. Smith departed April 14, 1860, and Michell gained the title of "acting surgeon."

Events took place in Tobias Michell's life that brought him to the attention of his superior, Abadie, Surgeon U.S.A. & Medical Director in

San Antonio, Texas. This officer wrote a letter to Brig. General Thos. Lawson, Surgeon General of the U. S. Army in Washington City, D. C. He discussed how Tobias Michell continued to perform the duty of a medical officer because a citizen physician could not be found. He also discussed a death in Michell's family by saying, "A few days since Dr. Michell having received the intelligence of the loss of a son, addressed the Colonel Comdg. urging that he might be relieved without delay, and that a leave be granted him under the circumstances of this bereavement." Michell was allowed to leave the post.

The surgeon writing this letter bemoaned the fact that two military posts, Camp Woods and Fort Chadbourne, were now without doctors. He said this would continue to be true until two doctors in the field returned from fighting the Comanches and Kiowas. He suggested that the Surgeon General should consider a list of approved candidates examined by the last board and contact them to fill the vacancies. Michell's superior was much more concerned about a need for doctors than for poor chaplains who performed a dual roll of preacher and physician.

Several years after Fort Chadbourne came into existence, a new fort appeared on the banks of the Concho River about forty miles south of Fort Chadbourne. Although the military called the new garrison "Fort Hatch" after its commander John Porter Hatch, it also carried the name "White City" because of the many tents. Eventually the War Department settled on the name Fort Concho to label this new home for the soldiers near the Concho River.

Rev. Norman Badger, one of the early chaplains at Fort Concho, arrived there in 1871. This fact is verified by the post surgeon's observation in April of that year. He said, "The Chaplain performed at Saint Angela probably the first time that the name of the Deity was ever publicly used in reverence in that place."

Badger seemed to care for the soldiers' welfare. He grew a vegetable garden for their use and also planned dances for the officers and men. Badger sent his periodic reports to his superior, the Right Reverend Robert Woodward Barnwell Elliott, Bishop of the Episcopal Church's Missionary District of Texas. After reading Badger's May 28, 1874, report, the Bishop thought there was hope for this western country because preachers now reported more marriages than before. In 1875 the Bishop visited Fort Concho and labeled Fort Concho the favorite garrison of West Texas.

Reverend Norman Badger, a chaplain at Fort Concho. Courtesy of the West Texas Collection at Angelo State University, San Angelo, Texas.

Bishop Elliott, in his many visits to forts, noticed very few preachers who maintained their holy calling in their desolate frontier environments, but he felt that Badger was different. In talking about Fort Concho the Bishop said, "Where it has a Chaplain who is also a churchman. Norman Badger, upon this outermost post, by his life and his teachings keeps before the eyes about him the great, living, saving facts of the gospel." Badger's good deeds came to a close as he died at Fort Concho June 3, 1876.

One challenge that all preachers experienced was fighting the shady side of life that most soldiers were exposed to in the wild towns that developed near the forts. Ft. Concho, near the Concho River, had to contend with the bad influences of St. Angela that sprouted up on the other side of the river. Fort Griffin had the Flat, hovels of degradation that emerged on an open space below the fort situated on top of a hill. The prostitutes and the card sharks enticed the soldiers to enjoy life away from the fort. Gamblers like Lottie Deno visited several forts in their lifetime.

Lottie Deno, a beautiful woman, was a professional gambler at Fort Griffin as well as Fort Concho. Courtesy of Fort Concho Historical Landmark.

Lottie Thompkins, later called Lottie Deno, was the daughter of wealthy parents and enjoyed traveling with her Dad to Europe at an early age. He loved to gamble at the finest casinos in the world, and Lottie accompanied him at a young age. Although she had been educated in the finest Christian schools, she soon learned to be a card shark herself.

Circumstances changed drastically for the young gambler when her father was killed in the Civil War. The management of the plantation fell into Lottie and her mother's hands. By the age of eighteen, Lottie was sent to Detroit to find a "proper" husband of the right social standing. However, Lottie found another man more to her liking.

She chased after a Jewish gambler named Johnny Golden. Lottie brought her nanny, a seven-foot-tall black woman named Mary Poindexter with her as she gambled. Lottie's Christian mother found out about this Jewish boyfriend and disowned her. Pretty Lottie, her companion and Johnny played cards up and down the Mississippi during the Civil War. Johnny eventually split, leaving Lottie and Mary to make traveling arrangements to San Antonio. Lottie later traveled to St. Angela near Fort Concho in the 1870s. She remained a recluse except when she donned her pretty gowns and held court at the gambling tables. So little was known about her that Lottie was known as "Mystic Maude."

Some lawmen liked her, but others thought she dipped into the brothel business as well as gambling. She left the Fort Concho area only to emerge one spring day of 1877 on the streets of the Flat near Ft. Griffin riding on top of the stage with the driver. Town people, who got a glimpse of her that day, thought she was beautiful. Whether in Fort Concho or Fort Griffin, Lottie Deno used those piercing black eyes and polished demeanor to her advantage. Fort chaplains tried in vain to keep soldiers from spending every dime of pay they had when women like Lottie made their appearance in the nearby saloons.

G. W. Dunbar, another chaplain at Fort Concho probably tried to discourage the troopers from playing cards when he preached there beginning September 30, 1877. He held services for the officers and their families whenever practical for the men and taught the officers' children on weekdays. Dunbar also held the offices of Fort Treasurer and Fort Librarian. He mentioned in his written monthly report to the Adjutant General's Office that he hoped there would be a fort garden next year.

When soldiers did get vegetables to enjoy from area farmers, they paid high prices. Occasionally, Dunbar made his wish list for the fort, and he always mentioned wanting a windmill. He thought such an addition to the Fort would be great to use in irrigating the garden.

On March 1, 1879, Fort Concho opened its post school. Dunbar mentioned in his reports that he directed the school, which was in a building forty feet by twenty feet in size. He called it the "best finished room in the Post." He added that the schoolroom made a good chapel also.

Dunbar used glowing terms to describe his school, but he had few materials with which to teach. He needed more books and furniture, items hard to come by. Sometimes when chaplains like Dunbar tried to teach the soldiers, his pupils fell asleep from exhaustion. Weary from a long day in the saddle, most soldiers found it hard to stay awake and recite their ABC's or calculate their sums.

But the War Department did not abandon the idea of teaching soldiers who could not read or write. In 1878 it published an order that listed the expectations they had for "persons responsible for operating post schools."

Colonel Alexander McCook, the first inspector of education, had an assistant named Chaplain George G. Mullins. These two men attempted to upgrade the Army's educational system as they rode from fort to fort. They also worked to improve post libraries and reading rooms.

Dunbar, stationed at Fort Concho, wrote home to his mother, Mrs. M. J. Dunbar in New York and described his surroundings. He praised the pure, clean air of West Texas. He also mentioned in his letter "the air tastes so good." He did not include the frequent sandstorms on the "tasty" list.

As if overseeing the school and the religious activities at Fort Concho was not enough to keep the parson busy, he had to check the bread making in the fort's kitchen also. In 1878 this garrison had a full house, so Kitchen Chief Dunbar had to be sure the ovens produced 400 loaves of bread every day. Dunbar was also the Fort Treasurer. In the letter to his mother, he said, "I handle over $200 of government money now." As to the length of his Sunday sermons, he mentioned that they had to be short—less than an hour.

Dunbar's wife and daughter Alice enjoyed activities with the women at the fort. He discussed his wife's frequent outings to fish with the other ladies along the Concho and play croquet at the Fort. His wife Addie had military blood running through her veins because her brother, General Rogers, carried the title of superintendent of West Point at one time.

Another minister directed to the same garrison, Rev. Frances H. Weaver, came to Fort Concho about 1879. He had many experiences at other places before he saw the pecan tree-lined waterways of the Concho Rivers in West Texas. Weaver, born in Pennsylvania in 1844, worked as a clerk for the War Department from 1864 to 1868. He changed his profession when he pastored churches in West Virginia in 1876–1877 and then became an army chaplain in 1879. His training was at the Theological Seminary in Gettysburg where he studied to be an Evangelical Lutheran minister.

When he officially received the title of chaplain, the army regulations stipulated that such ministers, "were to have the rank of captain without command and shall be on the same footing as other officers.

They must be a regular ordained minister and furnish proof of this before being appointed. They shall have at least a service on Sunday and be able to perform religious burial services."

When Weaver received orders to come to Fort Concho, he expected that his quarters would be ready by September 1882. Quarter #14, a nice two-storied limestone house, lay incomplete when the preacher arrived, so he had to live temporarily in the vacated home of Commander Benjamin Grierson. This situation was not satisfactory to the preacher, so he complained to the Post Adjutant.

He wrote a letter asking his superior to release the painter from all other duties until his house was completed. While his quarters were renovated, the chaplain received additional jobs. Weaver wore the title of Post Treasurer for a time as he counted money.

Little did Weaver know about earlier events that took place in Col. Benjamin H. Grierson's house. If he had known, he might have been scared to stay there at all while waiting for his house to be painted. On August 27, 1878, the Grierson's twelve-year-old daughter Edith fell ill with typhoid fever. Her body was racked with pain and high temperature as the disease took its course.

Mrs. Grierson telegraphed Fort Worth hoping to get some ice sent to San Angelo to cool her daughter's tongue, as well as her burning head. For thirteen days, the helpless parents watched their daughter grow weaker as she lay in the upstairs bedroom.

Edith passed away September 9, 1878. For many years afterward, visitors to that house, Officer Quarters #1, described sightings of apparitions, phantoms and phenomena such as doors slamming and locks turning for unknown reasons.

As recently as June 2003, a visitor staying in Quarters #1 described how she saw a figure descending the staircase about four o'clock in the morning. The ghost wore a pale peach dress. The visitor, Andrea Dominguez, said the figure looked like a girl about 12 years old who had long, light brown hair. The child left as silently as she came. When Andrea later saw a picture of Edith Grierson, she said, "She looks like the girl I saw."

As far as anybody knows, Parson Weaver never saw Edith nor her ghost. He came to Fort Concho August 3, 1882, accompanied by his wife Kate Schneider. Their arrival was four years after the girl's death.

Fort Concho, originated in 1867, was built along the Concho River. Courtesy of Fort Concho Historical Landmark.

Weaver also expounded on scriptures from the Good Book to the soldiers at Fort Davis, some two hundred miles southwest of Fort Concho. While living at the garrison near Limpia Canyon, Weaver's wife gave birth to a daughter named Marguerite and a son, Louis S.

Weaver served much later at Fort Davis than another preacher named Barr. Chaplain David E. Barr served at Fort Davis in the spring and summer of 1872. Since this fort had no schoolroom, Barr improvised. He used an outdoor classroom when possible. Beautiful cottonwood trees scattered around the parade ground made great places to sit in the shade and read Homer's *Iliad*. When showers swept over the Davis Mountains, the parson turned teacher moved his students into his own quarters.

Fort Davis had been in existence for eighteen years when Barr served at this garrison. In 1854, Capt. A. T. Lee led his troops to the foot of a mountain range that one day would protect Fort Davis on the west. The garrison took shape within a year and its soldiers helped guard travelers passing through the area on the Chihuahua Trail and the Butterfield Overland Mail Route. Settlers and travelers on the way to the Gold Rush in California also passed through this part of Texas. Troopers from Fort Davis were supposed to guard the six hundred miles of untamed wilderness from San Antonio to El Paso.

Before moving to Fort Davis, David Barr switched regiments several times. From 1865 to 1866, he was chaplain of the 81st U. S. Colored Infantry Regiment. He changed to the 39th Infantry when it was formed. Finally the 39th and 40th consolidated, and he was their chaplain in 1869. Barr was probably happy to settle down in Fort Davis for a while with the 25th Infantry. The Davis Mountains hovered over the camp as he slept in the rock officer quarters. Nearby Limpia Creek gurgled as it moved swiftly through the canyons and supplied adequate water for this fort.

While chaplains labored at their jobs at the forts, they often met opposition expressed openly by the men or by the officers. Learning about God Almighty was not high on the list of things soldiers wanted to do. What the average recruit at Fort Davis thought he needed was a chance to slip into one of the many saloons that existed nearby. Nearly every Texas fort had houses of ill repute as well as watering holes galore where a trooper could easily forget his troubles.

During this time, temperance societies swept the country, so chaplains urged soldiers to abstain from drinking. Preachers went so far as to urge the troopers to sign abstinence pledges. If the officer in command at the fort enjoyed a brandy or scotch from time to time, he did not appreciate the preacher's intentions either.

Rank was another area that separated the soldiers. Chaplains posted times for services and urged all soldiers to worship together. Because the military divided officers from noncommissioned officers and enlisted men in housing and other situations, it was difficult to get them to come together to pray or sing "Onward Christian Soldiers." Some officers resented that chaplains received a grade equivalent to captain. Regular soldiers thought that the preacher did not work as hard as the trooper did to get that rank.

Probably the chaplain figured he earned his rank double time. The preacher not only preached sermons to the soldiers, taught school, acted as a medical doctor and tallied the money as Fort Treasurer, he also ministered to men locked in the guardhouse. Some of these inmates who may have taken a swing at the new lieutenant, fresh out of West Point, were not ready to hear a chaplain discuss the verse from Corinthians, "Love is patient, love is kind."

Preachers also had to lead the song service. When early Texas Christians played the "Sacred Harp," they were really singing with their own voices. In the 1800s many churches had no instrument like a piano or an organ, but the people wanted to sing. There were few hymnals, and most churchgoers at that time did not know how to read music anyway.

Charles Wesley said, "The devil had all the good tunes." He took songs like "The Ballad of Captain Kidd" and added words to make it "Wondrous Love." "Auld Lang Syne" became the hymn "Hark! From the Tombs."

Another chaplain named Father Michael Sheehan made a long trip to the Lone Star State. He came from Ireland to Texas to take the job of fort chaplain. He served first in a Catholic church in Galveston in 1850. When he said Mass in Austin, Sheehan was preaching at the church he founded. Later he alternated services there with a trip to San Antonio where he preached also.

Although chaplains served at many forts, a group of militant protestors said that such preaching was not a true separation of church and state. They thought that no preaching about God should take place at United States forts. This uprising occurred in 1850, and again in 1853 and 1856. Father Michael Sheehan was in the middle of this controversy when he became chaplain at Fort Belknap in 1855.

Since this fort was established June 24, 1851, along the banks of the Brazos River, natural springs kept the men in plenty of drinking water. This location was eleven miles from present-day Graham. Although the first buildings were made of log, when Sheehan came to Belknap, he saw an array of pink sandstone barracks.

This fort was at the crossroads of activity. A stagecoach carried the mail, as well as passengers from Fort Belknap to Dallas. The Butterfield Overland Mail Company also directed its teams of horses or mules down the streets of Fort Belknap.

Since he was born in Ireland, Sheehan shared a special bond with some of the Irish soldiers stationed at Belknap. They could sing about the wearing of the green and tell stories about their beloved homeland. Sheehan continued to serve there until 1859. He may have traveled awhile at this time and returned to his homeland of Ireland. However, he eventually moved back to San Antonio where he had a sister living. He died there of apoplexy in 1889.

While Sheehan was a Catholic chaplain at Fort Belknap, Rev. David W. Eakin preached God's word at the same fort as a Presbyterian. Methodist preacher James Pleasant Tackitt lived near Fort Belknap and organized a church in the community but was never on the government payroll. But soldier and farmer both felt his leadership.

Tackitt, born in Kentucky April 22, 1803, began preaching as a Methodist in Arkansas in 1826. Keziah F. Bruton married this mountain man of a preacher in 1835, not knowing exactly the life she had signed up for. Otherwise, she might have thought twice about matrimony. Tackitt, assigned as a missionary by the Missouri Methodist Conference to the Cherokee Indians in Arkansas, acquired knowledge in 1829 that he would use later in life. He picked up some of the warriors' habits and part of their language.

The Reverend Tackitt continued to move westward until he and his family found themselves in Parker County, Texas, the spring of 1854. After he built a home for his family, Tackitt founded the Goshen Church and helped build an adjoining cemetery as well. Before he had a church building, he preached his first Texas sermon in Hezekiah Culwell's home.

His Methodist circuit included the communities of Goshen, Springtown and Ash Creek. The parson' circle of contacts stretched to Weatherford where he also organized the First Methodist Church of that town by 1857. The preacher's son, R. E. Tackitt, remembered that by the time they made it to Texas, troops removed from Fort Worth made their way to Fort Belknap in Young County. Most of the Indians were friendly with white people except a few renegades such as Chief Buffalo Hump, a Comanche warrior. From time to time he led a raid on isolated homes on the Texas frontier.

Since Tackitt had worked with the Cherokee earlier, he was appointed missionary to the Indians around Young and Shackleford counties. He had the responsibility of ministering to small tribes such as the Caddos, Wacos, Tonkawas, Anadarkos, Shawnees and a few Delawares. Because he preached to the Indians as well as the white settlers, Tackitt had a large circuit. His family remembered that Dad's circuit included 143 appointments at one time, which translated into a traveling distance of 1,200 miles to visit all of them.

Tackitt was a rustic, simple man. He wore homespun clothes that his wife made him and was his own cobbler. Many a night he slept outside under the stars when he was trying to get from one congregation to another. Some Indians in his area were not the friendly type that he saw in his Sunday services, a fact he would soon discover.

One day the Tackitt family member assigned to milk the cows in the evening, came to the barn. He noticed a cow of theirs walking along with an arrow sticking from its back. He reported the incident to his father who jumped into action. Fearing more problems with the Indians, Pleasant Tackitt took his three oldest sons, James, Lycurgus called "Like," and George with him to get the rest of their cattle. This hunting trip took place February 13, 1860. Each boy was armed with a gun as they searched for the cows around the area of Tackitt Mountain.

The men found the missing cattle and started home. Suddenly ten braves appeared from a ravine where they had waited to ambush the family. Arrows and bullets swished in the air as the battle commenced. When the weapons stopped firing, the Tackitts found four dead Indians and had some wounds of their own. James had an arrow lodged in his skull, and Pleasant had an arrow in his foot.

The men hobbled toward their house, but the Indians attacked them again about three hundred yards from home. As they squinted to see through the brush, they realized that the Indians had picked up additional help and were on higher ground. Knowing the warriors were so close to the Tackitt house scared the men because they were afraid the warriors had killed the rest of their family.

The Indians spooked the Tackitt's horses, so the animals ran toward the house. In all the confusion, the men outsmarted the Indians and slipped inside their home. All the family members were fine except the two injured boys. Once in the cabin, one of the brothers, Like, used a pair of shoemaker pinchers and tried to pull the spike out of Jim's face, but it would not budge.

As the family huddled inside the house, they listened to the Indians all night making sounds of barking dogs and owls hooting. For several days, the family melted snow for water rather than risking a trip to the creek. Finally the Indians became discouraged and left. Later the Tackitts discovered that the Indian charge had been lead by Comanche Piny Chummy.

Although Tackitt tried to preach God's love to the friendly Indians, he killed quite a few of those in this particular raiding band. He had the name of being the "fightin' parson" and was known to put notches on his gun to signify how many he killed.

On the calmer side, Pleasant Tackitt also held the title of Young County Chief Justice and postmaster. He led a full life as Texas preacher and was buried beside his wife, Keziah, in the Goshen Cemetery, five miles west of Springtown, in 1886.

Preachers who spread the gospel at the forts often found themselves holding down many jobs. They either lived outside the fort as Tackitt did, or they worked all the time inside its confines as chaplain, librarian, schoolteacher, doctor and treasurer or cook. The life of a chaplain was never boring, to say the least. Neither were the lives of preachers who dared to ride the lonesome trails into the Texas panhandle.

9

PREACHERS IN THE
PANHANDLE: 1870–1900s

When circuit riders finally got to the Panhandle of Texas they found it harbored a mixture of souls. As the Civil War ended, more preachers came out of the South. Some men of God, disillusioned with the carpetbagger government, headed west like other Confederate sympathizers. Most of these parsons were saints, but some got into trouble, some cared more for the dollar than for God's blessings, and one swung by the end of a rope.

Many of the preachers coming to the northwest corner of Texas were not prepared for what they experienced. They found either gospel citadels like Clarendon with seven Methodist ministers, not to mention the many other preachers; or they found "sin cities" like Tascosa. Between the two towns were miles and miles of no-man's-land.

If preachers visited Tascosa in the northwest portion of the Panhandle in the 1870s, they would think they were walking the streets of Monterrey, Mexico, instead of Texas. A sheepherder named Casimero Romero brought a group of his people, along with the sheep, to the banks of the Canadian River in 1876. These first residents of the Tascosa area were determined to survive the dust storms and chilling winds of winter.

They fashioned adobe bricks from dirt and grass, a task they knew well from the old country. Snug adobe huts protected them from the northern gales that swept over the prairies.

The Mexicans knew how to adapt in this land far from their comfortable haciendas in Mexico. When they saw the water in the nearby Canadian River, they built earthen dams and irrigation ditches to water their fields. Mexican freighters also directed their ox carts through this region as they provided goods for ranchers and military posts in the New Mexico region.

The tranquil countryside with bleating woolies and small green patches of cornfields eventually had noisy company. Bawling cattle found their way northward on the Tascosa–Dodge City Trail, accompanied by some equally noisy cowboys shooting up the town. Bible-toting preachers did not usually accompany the trail drives.

The cattle-driving visitors changed Tascosa drastically. In a short time, its citizens saw thirsty cowhands coming through town bent on drinks aplenty and having a good time. These sun-baked men did not know the words "quiet" and "tranquil."

If a preacher stepped into the street to mentioned God, his Bible would be nothing more than a target for some six-gun shooter. Cowboys let the bullets fly as they rode through the streets announcing their arrival in town. Tascosa transformed itself from a few adobe huts to many wooden stores facing the streets. After growing in numbers, Tascosa became the county seat of Oldham County in 1880. Saloons cropped up on every corner of the community, along with general stores and blacksmiths.

With the thundering herds came lawlessness, so Caleb Berg "Cape" Willingham pinned a sheriff's badge on his shirt and walked Tascosa streets as its first lawman. Willingham had the illustrious title of having killed the first man who occupied Tascosa's Boot Hill Cemetery. Other outlaws followed the trail to Tascosa as Billy the Kid and Dave Rudabaugh showed their faces walking the dusty streets of this Panhandle town. Sheriff Willingham had company when lawmen Pat Garrett and Charles Siringo spent some time on the high plains looking for fugitives from the law. All this lawlessness bothered the quieter sheepherders, so most of the Mexican citizens of Tascosa left the area and moved to New Mexico.

When gunfighters like Billy the Kid, Bat Masterson and Dave Rudabaugh sauntered down the streets of Tascosa, someone always managed to start a pistol-shooting contest. One day in 1879, lawyer Temple Houston, Sam Houston's son, happened to be in town. The promoters of the marksmanship contest tried to interest everybody in competing, but those cowboys who knew anything about shooters left the contest to Billy and Temple.

As the story goes, Billy the Kid came to the Panhandle in 1878 after John Chisum sent some of his cattle from his New Mexico ranch to graze the Canadian Valley. Chisum did not employ Billy. Instead, he and some friends had 125 stolen horses in their possession, which they hoped to sell to the Texas cowboys.

Temple Houston was just a year older than Billy the Kid even though their pasts were quite different. Temple Houston may have lost his father, Sam Houston, when he was only three, but he was a big, raw-boned cowboy who looked grown at thirteen. At that age he worked the round-ups and followed the cattle trails northward. Temple used his dead father's influence to become a U.S. Senate page when he was fifteen. While working in the Washington offices, he studied law and passed the bar exam at the age of eighteen.

This young man who had an aura of leadership about him much like his father returned to the Texas coast and began practicing law. Temple was elected district attorney of some coastal counties at a young age. He was in control wherever he was, whether it was in the courtroom or on the side streets.

He traveled from the saltwater regions westward and found himself visiting Tascosa's saloons. This trip may have been a vacation Temple enjoyed before he took over the serious job of district attorney. Everyone declined to shoot against these two, Billy the Kid and Temple Houston, even Bat Masterson. The latter realized he was too slow for these two gunslingers, so he maneuvered the contest to a place near the river and behind the saloons. Masterson threw a plug of tobacco up in the sky, and Temple cut loose with his pistol. He shot the tin star off the plug from twenty yards. Even the Kid was impressed and declined to duplicate the fine exhibition put on by Temple Houston.

Such shooting matches or other lawlessness were unheard of in Clarendon, a town about forty miles south of present-day Pampa. This community was the brainchild of a Methodist minister named Rev. Lewis Henry Carhart. The parson and his brother-in-law, Alfred Sully of New York, made big plans. The two men purchased railroad land scrip, which enabled them to have 343 sections of Texas turf. By 1878 Carhart and Sully brought in big investors such as an English firm named the Clarendon Land Investment and Agency Company to back the new town with money.

Some people believed that this group of men from England named the town Clarendon because of their company name. Others think the town was named for Carhart's wife, Clara.

The only way that Clarendon was connected to Tascosa was by their stagecoach line. A man could ride from Tascosa to Clarendon, but he might not like the contrast between the two towns. During its early years, Clarendon had no saloons. Carhart developed his "Christian Colony" and managed to bring a lot of people to his town. In addition to regular businesses flourishing, Clarendon's inhabitants also built churches and planned schools. W. A. Allen, another brother-in-law of Carhart, started a Methodist College in this nice town described as "a sobriety settlement."

As Clarendon grew, some of its inhabitants decided they wanted a little variety in life. They built a saloon. It was followed by a "gambling den," and both places of iniquity were located in the Feather Hill section of town. Two powerful forces worked against them. Frequent prayer meetings and strong law enforcement brought a change. These businesses of ill repute were closed down and taken away by 1898. The Holy Book still had influence in Clarendon.

While some preachers developed towns, others got themselves in big trouble. A preacher named G. E. Morrison, a resident of Panhandle City in Carson County, strayed from the holy teachings when he fell in love with a woman who was not his wife. Rev. Morrison was not a pistol-packing preacher, he was a poison-packing preacher. When Mrs. Morrison suddenly died, evidence indicated that she met her demise with the aid of strychnine. Morrison was tried in Vernon because of a change in venue. When prosecutors described the evidence they possessed in the case, the jury declared Morrison guilty of murder on October 10, 1899.

Although the preacher Morrison was guilty, some of the citizens did not want to see him hang for his deeds. Two attorneys and Morrison's sister went so far as to plead with Texas Governor J. D. Sayers to commute the preacher's sentence to life imprisonment. Their pleas had some effect on the governor. Years later Governor Sayers described the incident. Sayers said that when the visitors begged for Morrison's life, he gave some thought to changing the sentence.

On Oct. 25, 1899, Morrison had his sister interceding for him in the governor's office when he decided to try a jailbreak. The preacher and two fellow prisoners attacked jailer C. C. Shive. While the jailer was manhandled, Morrison yelled, "Kill the jailer." When this incident was reported to the governor, he sent a telegram to Sheriff J. T. Williams telling him to proceed with the hanging Oct. 29, 1899.

W. J. L. Sullivan, a Texas Ranger, was asked by Sheriff Williams to help with the hanging. The Sheriff said such events were troublesome to him. The lawmen admitted he could fire a gun at a man a lot easier than he could hang him. A large crowd came to view the event on the appointed day. Morrison's sister, a preacher and another woman visited the convicted man in jail before the execution, and the jailer said they prayed together.

On the day of the hanging, Morrison stood on the scaffold at twelve noon, made a farewell speech and then fell through the trap door as his rope tightened about his neck. Thus ended the only legal hanging in Wilbarger County. Before the event, Texas Ranger Sullivan asked Morrison to write him a note. The preacher obliged by giving him a letter as well as a pair of suspenders and a matchbox. The condemned man explained in his letter that he had committed a sin for which he was being punished. Morrison believed that although God would judge him for killing his wife, God would also save him.

Although some preachers were bad, most of them were bent on doing God's will. Robert Dunn who rode across the Panhandle plains was one such parson. This minister spent his childhood far away from the Panhandle of Texas. As a youngster of six years of age, Dunn heard war tales told by his father, a member of Gen. J. E. B. Stuart's cavalry fighting for the South. The sound of soldiers' shooting came nearer to his home until he witnessed actual battles. The fighting was so close to Dunn there in Virginia that his first memory of life was shooing the hogs off of corpses after a nearby conflict.

Reconstruction days were rough on families like the Dunns. However, when his father decided to move the family from Virginia to Texas, it was no picnic either. Boys like Robert Franklin Dunn walked the dusty trail behind the family's wagon every step of the way into the Lone Star State in 1873. Dunn's family hoped that Texas was to be the land of promise, so they stopped in Stephenville. As they worked outside on their farm, the family saw Indians, lots of Indians. In later years, Dunn said, "It must have been the fervent prayer of a righteous man, my dad, that saved our scalps."

Dunn's parents urged the children to get an education. That lesson sat well with Robert Dunn because as soon as he was old enough, he attended Granbury College in Hood County and graduated in 1882. This school had been under the leadership of the Methodist Episcopal Church South since 1880 and had both elementary and high school classes.

When David Switzer became head of Granbury College in 1880, the classes not only included lower-level courses, but also included some college level. Dunn was ordained a Methodist minister at this time and taught Greek at his alma mater for several semesters. But there was one more title he wanted, that of husband. He married Luella Spruill June 21, 1882. Granbury College combined with Weatherford College in 1884 and moved to that town, so Dunn became a full-time circuit rider.

He and his family decided to follow the Texas and Pacific Railroad as it inched its tracks westward. Robert Dunn received his first assignment as a circuit rider in the Sweetwater District, a little district that stretched from Sweetwater to Tascosa in the Panhandle, a distance of about 230 miles. Church buildings were noticeably absent from the scenery of the never-ending prairies facing the Dunn family.

The loneliness that Robert Dunn's family felt was countered by the closeness of Robert, Luella and the children. They prayed together, studied the Bible and sang religious songs. One of their children said, "I thought 'Shall We Gather at the River' was the national anthem until I was grown and left home."

Since Dunn was the first preacher in this area looking for a place to talk about the Holy Book, he preached anywhere he could, including the Colorado City Saloon. At this time, they had plenty of "watering holes" in this community, twenty-eight to be exact. Oddly enough, the owner of the Colorado City Saloon wanted the parson to preach in his establishment. Prayers by his aging mother were ringing in the saloonkeeper's ears, and he wanted to follow her teaching.

Colorado City was not very permanent in 1881, for even the grocery store was a dugout with logs completing the aboveground portion.

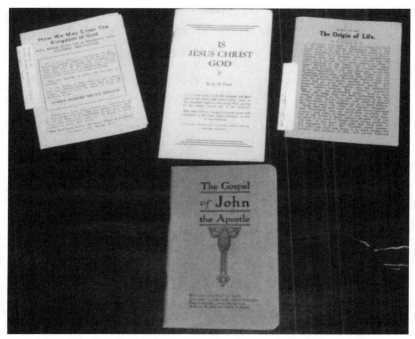

Pamphlets found in Circuit Rider Joseph Manning Berry's saddlebags. He preached in the 1880s. From left to right the titles are How We May Enter the Kingdom of God, Is Jesus Christ God?, *and* The Origin of Life. *Front center is* The Gospel of John the Apostle. *Courtesy of First Methodist Church of San Angelo's Archives.*

The store had tent material for a roof. Most everyone lived in a tent. One street alone had five hundred tents flapping in the breeze.

Once the Dunn family was relatively secure in Colorado City, the reverend packed his Bible with a few clothes in his saddlebags and pointed his horse toward various communities in the Panhandle. He made his complete circuit four times during the year. This trip included Denver, Colorado, to the north, San Angelo to the south, Abilene to the east and El Paso to the west. His sorrel horse took him over the plains so he could preach the Good News many times in dugouts, on ranches, at an isolated settler's homestead or under brush arbors.

Dunn's travels brought him to rough towns like Tascosa, and at other times, he found himself riding great distances to find a lonely homestead, but the devil did not have any fence lines. People needed to hear God's word no matter how isolated they were, or if they were living in Tascosa.

Indians were an ever-present danger as Dunn tried to carry out his job. When he finally had quite a few members scattered across the Panhandle, he decided to have a church conference. Preachers from all around the area came, but while they were conducting church business, they had visitors. The Indians stole all their horses. By this time, the warriors were supposed to be contained in the Indian Territory northeast of the Panhandle, but war parties of braves would burst out of confinement as the mood struck them and ride the plains once more. The preacher's mounts looked like as good a horseflesh to steal as any other.

When Robert Dunn and his horses were both worn out from too many miles, the circuit was divided. Rev. J. T. Bludworth took over the Panhandle half of the circuit, and Dunn preached in the lower half. Dunn started the first churches in Sweetwater, Colorado City, Big Springs and Snyder.

Some circuit-riding preachers kept their noses out of the cowman's business, but others knew what was going on during the roundups. A few cowboys were not exactly honest when it came time to mark the calves belonging to the ranch for which they worked. Preachers of God's word also knew that some horse thieves were known to find their rope around another man's horse.

J. Frank Dobie in his book, *Cow People*, described life in the northwestern side of Texas. He said one Panhandle preacher was letting his congregation know what ways God did or did not want a Christian cowboy to act when he told his congregation, "Some of your freshly branded calves don't suck the right cows."

Along with Dunn, another preacher who headed west was Peter Gravis. Maybe life was too exciting in Central Texas for circuit riders like Peter Gravis. Something caused him to move to the Panhandle District a few years after the Comanche County shootings. Now he could feel the dust storms and see the huge open plains. On one trip through his district, Gravis traveled for 100 miles on the cattle trail and passed at least three herds going north. This preacher spent so many nights under the stars by the road that he had a name for his accommodations, the Sprawls and Bowers Hotel. On one trip he let the cattle herd ford the river before he and his wife crossed in their buggy. After 600 steers crossed the river, the shore was very slick and messy. Their buggy went into the water without any trouble, but when the horse tried to climb out onto the far shore, it was so slippery and muddy that they fell back into the river. After the horse tried to climb out unsuccessfully several times, cowboys grabbed the harness and helped the buggy horse pull the parson and his wife out of the water.

Indians seemed always to be just around the corner from where Peter Gravis lived. Warriors visited him regularly in the Panhandle as they escaped the Indian Territory and raided through the countryside. Gravis, talking about this wild area of Texas said, "We should leave it to them."

By 1881, the Panhandle District was dissolved because the missionary treasury was empty. Even so, Gravis continued the next ten years traveling and preaching at camp and quarterly meetings. He and Mary watched their ten children mature and leave home. Mary died in 1885, and in later years, Gravis lived with his daughter Ella. He wrote his autobiography, which was a small pamphlet that he sold for twenty-five cents. The general feeling among friends was that he wrote it so that he and Ella would have some income. Gravis passed away on January 18, 1902, at Zephyr in Brown County.

Another preacher who headed his wagons westward was George Slaughter. He had freighted for Sam Houston as a young man, preached in East Texas, and now moved his cattle from Freestone County to Palo Pinto County in 1857. This man had a hard time completing all his chores in twenty-four hours because he preached, farmed, ranched and practiced medicine. Six hundred head of longhorns traveled to Central Texas with Slaughter and his family.

With this many cattle the parson needed land and extra cowboys. His son, Christopher Columbus, was twenty years old at this time, and he was his father's right-hand man. Slaughter realized that the open spaces he saw in this high plains area would soon be gobbled up by land-hungry settlers. Near Golconda, Slaughter purchased 2,000 acres of ranch land.

He tried to farm in that area for about a year and then decided to move his cattle to a ranch in Young County, northwest of Fort Worth. This location was near the Ross Indian Reservation. Since his herd had increased to 1,200 head, along with quite a few horses, he had unfriendly neighbors eyeing his ponies. In 1860 Indians successfully stole about

George W. Slaughter freighted for Sam Houston and preached from East Texas to the Panhandle. Courtesy of the Southwest Collection/Special Collection Library, Texas Tech University, Lubbock, Texas, SWCPC 154-E10.

forty head. This act was so common that the government later paid him, as well as other Texas ranchers, Indian Depredation funds. He received a total of $6,500 for his stolen livestock over a period of time.

During these years, Preacher Slaughter would often saddle his horse, fill his saddlebags with hard tack as well as cans of peaches and maybe some bacon, grab his picket rope and arm himself with two six-shooters to assist his rifle. This Baptist circuit rider would traverse distances of sixty miles or more between his parishioners. Although Indians attacked him twice while he was alone, he managed to evade them successfully.

Slaughter helped his neighbors not only with their religious problems but also when they were sick or hurting. The fact that he had studied medicine along with his preaching and driving cattle became useful. He was the only physician in the isolated areas along the open plains, so he was very welcome in the sick room even though his diploma from medical school may have been missing. Slaughter bound the wounds of the hurting when he could, as well as helped the needy with his time and his cash.

George Slaughter had several close encounters with the Indians. In 1864 he opened fire on seven Indians while he was riding along Cedar Creek in Palo Pinto County. They traded shots, and the Indians rode away. He was also attacked on Dry Creek near Graham in 1866. Slaughter was driving a small herd of cattle and had to open fire on the warriors to protect himself. He wounded one Indian, and the other warriors disappeared. In 1867 Indians raided his ranch and not only stole all his horses but also shot his son, John Slaughter, in the breast.

Sometimes the Indians attacked government teamsters, as they did in April 1869. The warriors killed all thirteen of the men. George Slaughter was only two miles from this massacre holding 800 head of cattle, but this time Slaughter had fourteen men with him. He was clever in outwitting the Indians when he saw them approaching his herd. Slaughter sent the cattle in the direction of Sand Creek with six cowboys. The other eight men prepared for the oncoming Indians. Using a ravine nearby, some of the cowboys slipped away and appeared to the Indians at a different place. The braves thought these men were reinforcements for the cowboys, so they left in a hurry.

Slaughter's son Christopher wanted to strike out as a young twenty-year-old and make money on his own. But C. C., as he was nicknamed, was so poor he did not have money for a saddle. Rather than spend money on one, he rode bareback. To make a few bucks, C. C. bought a load of cow and buffalo hides and freighted them all the way to Jefferson. This trip took him to the land of steamboats. Before he headed west, he bought some merchandise that he peddled on the return trip through Dallas and Palo Pinto.

As his father's holdings increased, C. C. found himself fully employed by his preacher dad. The first time the young cowboy received a month's wages, his thoughts drifted toward saddles. However, the money could also be used to buy cattle, and that is the decision he finally made. Once he had to help roundup when all the neighbors got together, but he still had no saddle. He was teased a bit, but he never fell off even though some renegade cows had him popping through the brush at a pretty fast tempo.

Once the Civil War was over, Texas cattle began to move up the trails most often to Kansas. In 1868, Slaughter sold 12,000 cattle to James Loving and Charles Rivers at a price of $6 a head. The parson decided there was money to be made by driving cattle northward to the railheads, so he formed a partnership with his son, C. C. Slaughter. Their first endeavor was a small herd of 800 head, and these cattle brought $32,000 in Kansas. Most of the livestock that made it this far were shipped on to St. Louis and Chicago. The preacher's family continued to drive herds for seven years northward to the railheads. In 1870, the Slaughters sold 3,000 head for $105,000 and another herd for $75,000.

As George Slaughter visited Kansas, he could see that children had more opportunities in that civilized area than they did in the Panhandle of Texas, so he moved his family to Emporia, Kansas, in 1870. Some unmentioned factors must have pulled him back to Texas pretty soon because the entire Slaughter clan returned to the ranch in Palo Pinto County in 1875. The parson continued to trail herds northward, but after 1876, he dissolved his partnership with C. C. and entered an agreement with another son named Peter. They shipped cattle together until 1884 when the old cowboy decided to quit going up the trail. His bad health was slowing him down.

George Slaughter was ever on the run, but he managed to witness to many people along the way. As a Baptist minister, he claimed to have baptized 3,000 people, ordained more preachers, and organized more churches than anybody in the state.

The Slaughter family was blessed with eleven children. As George lay on his sick bed and realized his life was near its end, he was surrounded by six of his children, as well as his good friend, Rev. Rufus C. Burleson of Waco. Rev. George Slaughter passed away March 19, 1895.

Although Slaughter was no longer punching cattle, his sons were deep into the ranching business. C. C. noticed a pretty young lady named Cynthia Anne Jowell, who lived near Palo Pinto. Even though her family lived in a modest cabin, Cynthia had the important traits: she could ride, shoot and dance, not to mention her beauty, which C. C. noticed right away.

The parson's son courted and married Cynthia, and they rode back into the hills where their first little cabin was situated. She did fine until C. C. was away one day and the Indians approached their house. Cynthia bolted the door, but the Indians begged for food. She opened the door a crack to push the food out to them. When an Indian lunged through the door, she shot him. The other warriors left, but when C. C. returned, he was shocked to see a dead Indian on his doorstep.

Cynthia and C. C. survived the weather and warriors to live their complete life in that area. At one time they owned a million acres and were the biggest taxpayers in Texas.

Another preacher who went westward was J. L. Pyle. He lived along the Prairie Dog Town Fork of the Red River where it meanders through Hall County. The parson owned land two miles north of the river where the town Plaska originated. In 1900 he moved near Newlin and lived in a dugout. This seemed like an odd location for a publisher, but Pyle produced the bimonthly newsletter *Panhandle Baptist*. Pyle had a female typesetter who made the paper a reality, but when she quit to get married, he could not find a replacement. Before very long, Pyle grew weary of typesetting, so the paper was no longer printed.

The town of Newlin where Pyle lived got its name from W. J. Newlin. He was a man who camped with Col. Charles Goodnight and Emanuel E. Dubbs in the valley near this future town site.

Pyle found himself in an argument between the citizens of Newlin and those of Memphis, which was the county seat started in 1889. Although the train tracks ran near the town of Memphis, the train did not stop there nor was there a depot at this county seat. Some citizens thought the locomotive should make a stop in Memphis. These people were so mad that they smeared lye soap on the tracks near Newlin. The engineer got a surprise on his next trip through the town. He could not stop the train. Finally in 1892 the officials of the railroad company made a deal to build a depot in Memphis. A new courthouse appeared there the same year. Pyle organized a Missionary Baptist Church in Memphis and spent most of his time preaching to congregations scattered throughout the area.

Other preachers helped to spread the gospel in Texas. Rev. Cal Wright also rode the circuits of the Panhandle. He felt that the $121 salary he received per year needed supplementing to survive. Wright knew how to work cattle much as Slaughter did. Since he was friendly with the cowboys of that region, he helped them during spring branding season. One ranch where he liked to rope calves was the T-Bar in southern Lynn County, which would be halfway between modern-day Lubbock and Lamesa. He could often be seen working the roundups for this outfit.

The people who heard Wright's messages were few and far between, ranch houses, that is. He said, "Once I got lost when trying to find a certain place on a dark Sunday night. I rode all night. After that, the ranchers would place lighted kerosene lanterns on the windmill towers if I was due in a certain place."

Cal Wright loved his faithful flock even if he had to endure sandstorms, droughts and sometimes talking to folks who had imbibed in the spirits a little too much. One night he heard a knock at his door and opened it to see two rather drunk cowboys. They knew their predicament because they told him they needed his prayers. In fact they asked him how much he charged to pray for them. Wright replied that $10 ought to do the job. He prayed, and they thanked him and left. The following day, Wright met one of the cowboys in the street. The rather sober fellow asked the preacher what he was going to do with the ten dollars he gave him. Wright answered that he intended to give it to a woman with children who had been deserted by her husband. It was Christmas time, and the preacher surmised she could use it to buy presents for the family. When the cowboy heard this tale, he gave the parson $100 more.

Drought could take a cattleman out of business quicker than anything else. For that reason, prayer meetings were well attended when the main focus of the group was praying for rain. One such get-together by ranching families was held in a Panhandle school building. The conversation turned to the power of prayer in changing the weather. One rather closed-lipped rancher surprised everybody by speaking out rather bluntly. He said, "I don't mind praying, but I can tell you right now it won't do a damned bit of good as long as this dry wind stays in the west."

Besides praying for rain, many country preachers had a favorite topic to pray against. They were outspoken about prohibition. One night a circuit-riding minister launched into his pray-for-rain meeting in a ranching area where he had often extolled about the sins of drinking. His words had made a few cowboys angry.

One night he jumped into one of his prayers for rain when he saw several cowboys coming into the room with their slickers still on. They made a spectacle of themselves by sitting in the front row. The preacher got rather hot under the collar when they appeared. He tried to go on with the meeting only to hear someone laughing. He grew more belligerent and asked the cowboys to leave. They turned to him and said, "We just came prepared for the rain."

Just as cowboys did not care for prohibitionists, they also did not care for people who preached new theologies about religion. One cowman questioned the new theory, and the preacher was irate. He said, "Now, I'd like to know who you are to be questioning me?"

The cowman replied, "Who am I? I'll tell you who I am. I am a follower of the meek and lowly Jesus. I say to hell with this newfangled theology."

Cowboys did not always get to hear church music and preachers. Most of their days they were calming a herd without having pens for them. Cattle would become settled more at night if a cowboy would sing to them. According to one observer of cattle herds, some animals had a preference for certain songs.

There was a particular Texas longhorn known to react to certain songs that the cowboys sang at night. When this animal heard "Jesus, Lover of my Soul," he would get up from where he had been resting and stretch out his neck.

Preachers figured out pretty quickly that humans were a lot like that longhorn. In 1889, a Texas preacher named Bro. Butterfield was holding a revival and leading the music as well as preaching. He successfully led the crowd in "Jesus Saves" and "Almost Persuaded," but he needed one more altar-calling song. He was almost without a voice and could not decide what to do.

He wanted one more song that usually brought the sinners to the mourning bench, but he was out of air and out of any ideas. Just when he thought the service was a lost cause, a cowboy suddenly began to sing, "Oh, Bury Me Not on the Lone Prairie." That set the mood, and mourners began to hit the sawdust trail. They came forward to give Butterfield their hands and give themselves to Jesus.

With ranch houses scattered a great distance apart, towns were created at a slow pace. Lubbock was finally incorporated as a town in 1909. The Methodist congregation organized there in 1892, but the people had no building in which to meet. City fathers were helpful and let them meet awhile in the schoolhouse and later in the courthouse.

Anyone who had traveled in that area of Texas knew that Lubbock had no lumber or lumber mills. The nearest town that provided such material was Colorado City, so it took awhile to freight the boards that far.

Missions like this Methodist church in Lubbock were called "Coldwater Missions" because they had no church house, no parsonage and no parish. Usually young inexperienced preachers were sent to the less desirable circuits to preach the gospel. However, in 1900 W. B. McKeown preached the Coldwater Mission in the Panhandle region. His district included six Panhandle counties. A friend looked at this desolate area and told McKeown, who had previously been a college president, "Mac, the bishop has given you a bunghole, and he expects you to build a barrel around it." McKeown went to work with surprising gusto and developed his circuit.

Most of the Panhandle preachers never expected a big congregation. They just followed the Lord's lead and ministered to people where they found them. Another group of God's messengers, the priests, did not expect big crowds either. They started along the Rio Grande riding their donkeys and spread their message throughout Texas.

10

THE PADRES SPREAD
GOD'S MESSAGE: 1600–1900s

In the early 1800s, the padres spread God's message from the Gulf of Mexico, up the winding Rio Grande and across Texas's lonely prairies to its many forts. Although the most familiar sight would be a padre, wearing his black habit, walking or riding a donkey down a dusty trail, one padre looked more like a cattleman as he rode across his large ranch.

Father Balli was that priest herding cattle, which made for an interesting situation. Jose Nicolas Balli led a charmed life as both priest and ranch owner. He was born in Reynosa, Mexico, about 1770, to Jose Maria and Rosa Maria Hinojosa de Balli. His early years were carefree as he enjoyed the life of the affluent. Among his many blessings, Balli counted an education from elite schools as well as having all he wanted to eat and plenty of this world's goods. His parents owned over a million acres in Reynosa, Camargo, Matamoros and the Lower Rio Grande Valley. When Balli told stories of his boyhood, they included life in Reynosa with his younger brothers, Juan Jose and Jose Maria Balli. Later he left home and attended the Conciliar Catholic Seminary in Monterrey to finish his secondary, as well as ecclesiastical, education.

As Nicolas Balli held Catholic services in villas and haciendas in the Lower Rio Grande Valley, he also found time to ranch and explore South Texas. Probably because he had businesses as well as church activities, Balli was called a secular minister. He was the official priest of Nuestra Senora del Refugio Mission in Matamoros from 1804 to 1829. As if Balli did not wear enough hats, he also shouldered the responsibility of collecting funds for new churches up and down the Rio Grande. He also began the construction of the present Catholic Church in Matamoros.

Balli could have spent all his time with his real estate because he owned Spanish Land Grants including the La Feria, the Las Castanas, part of the Llano Grande and the Isla de Santiago. All of these land titles he received were part of the famous Spanish Land Grants given to his fore-bears.

One grant became known as Padre Island, named after Father Nicolas Balli. His grandfather received this land from King Carlos III of Spain in 1759, but nobody in the family had asked for a clear title. Balli set the wheels in motion to get the sandy beach put in his name in 1827. He encouraged new families to live by the sea, and he built a church for the island's occupants of many years, the Karankawa Indians.

The meaning of this tribal name, Karankawa, is not certain, but most people think it means "dog lovers" or "dog raisers" because they were known to have fox-like or coyote-like dogs. Since the Karankawas lived on the islands or near the Gulf of Mexico, their main diet consisted of fish, shellfish and turtles. These Indians were gatherers, so they probably had a variety of plants and animals that made their way into the cooking pot. When they wanted hot water, they used hot stones dropped into a water-filled hide container to boil water and cook their food.

This group of Indians defended their territory by killing settlers such as the Flowers and Cavanah women. In the winter of 1826–1827, the Karankawa massacred Polly Flowers and Cavanah's wife, along with three daughters. These families lived on Liveoak Bayou. However, in May 1827, Jacob Betts and some other colonists signed a peace treaty with these Indians at La Bahia. This group of poor, ill-equipped Indians could not compete with the white colonists who flooded into Texas, so the Karankawas became extinct by 1858.

Padre Nicolas wanted a town on the island, so he founded El Ran-cho Santa Cruz de Buena Vista, later called the Lost City. Nicolas kept his livestock, cattle, horses and mules near this town. On April 16, 1829, the weary padre died as he approached the age of sixty. The title to his island was granted to him eight months after his death. Nicolas had ear-lier paid $460 for this island of 340,000 acres. His nephew, Juan Jose Balli, received half of the island at the time of his uncle's death and lived there until his own passing in 1853.

In 1847, Padre Island was uninhabited until John Singer, his wife and four children washed ashore after a shipwreck. Padre Nicolas Bali's headquarters were covered with mountains of sand by this time, so the family had no house to use. When the Singer family set foot on this sandy beach, their wealth from their Singer Sewing Machine Company gave them no added advantage.

They made the best of the isolated situation by building a house and corrals out of mahogany pieces of shipwreck. The island was filled with wild cattle and horses, so the Singer family became ranchers out of necessity. The Singer cowboys branded about 1,500 calves each year.

Tropical storms brought more ship debris that the exiles could examine. One kind of trash the Singer family particularly liked were the boxes of jewelry and gold. Before the family left Padre Island, they buried about $80,000 in gold and silver. Years later they returned to claim their bounty but were never able to find the treasure. During the Civil War, Union troops stationed on the island consumed the entire Singer herd and destroyed the mahogany ranch house. The padre's island witnessed one disaster after another.

Even though Padre Balli was deceased, his nephews lived in the area. The Balli name continued to represent men of affluence as Don Francisco Balli's children married scrappy Anglo settlers in that region of the Rio Grande Valley. One daughter, Maria Salome, married John McAllen, an immigrant from Ireland. He became judge of Hidalgo County, the most powerful position of that area. According to his descendant, James A. McAllen, "By 1865, Maria and John had 1,800 head of cattle, which made their ranch one of the largest Hispanic-owned spreads north of the border."

John McAllen understood trade, even during the Civil War. At that time, England needed cotton to aid its industrial revolution, and McAllen could provide it. After building the first cotton gin in the Rio Grande Valley, he managed to avoid the Union blockades by floating his cotton bales across the Rio Grande. Then from a Mexican port, he shipped the needed fiber to Baghdad.

McAllen's exporting colleagues also devised a way to import weapons they could sell to the Confederacy at inflated prices. If Union soldiers passed through his ranch, McAllen would just as easily sell them supplies as he would the Confederates. This rancher was a survivor, so he had no qualms about taking advantage of either side—North or South.

The present-day San Juanito Ranch in the Rio Grande Valley is a testimony to Father Balli's, as well as John McAllen's, influence in the ranching industry. But other priests rode the Rio Grande Valley trails also and possessed only the clothes on their back.

Many priests had a longer trip to their Texas parish than Padre Nicolas Balli did. Although Eugene de Mazenod established the Missionary Oblates of Mary Immaculate, which sent priests to the shores of Texas, this priest was heard to moan, "Cruel Texas Mission." From his office in France, Mazenod sent forty-one young padres to Texas. He mourned for his fellow men of God because life was hard in this region of the New World. His priests met outlaws along the border and traversed hot, lonely trails as well as experienced yellow fever and hurricanes. Two priests were forcibly removed from Ciudad Victoria in 1860. Three padres found themselves in prison at Matamoros during Benito Juarez's era and seven oblates died from 1853 to 1862.

This saga of the Oblate Fathers in Texas began in 1849 when Bishop Jean Marie Odin assigned the oblates a region of eight of the southernmost counties of Texas. These circuit riders, dressed in their black soutanes with the oblate cross hung from their neck, directed their horses or donkeys to the remote ranches and villages of that region. Often the Fathers would go a hundred miles or more in a six-weeks circuit around the cactus- and mesquite-infested area. Each padre was special in some way.

Father Keralum could hear confessions or ply his trade as an architect. Pierre Yves Keralum, born in Quimper, Brittany, France, on March 2, 1817, never thought about traveling to America. Instead, he made plans to take a different direction in his life. Keralum wanted to build houses and other structures, so he became a journeyman carpenter and architect. Just when his future seemed to be on course, he would get these nagging urges in his soul to enter the priesthood. Finally, as a twenty-eight-year-old man, he gave in to the calling and entered the Diocesan Seminary of Quimper.

Five years later, after much study and meditation as a deacon, he was accepted into the missionary congregation of the Oblates of Mary Immaculate. Keralum had the distinct pleasure of being ordained by the congregation's founder, Bishop de Mazenod, on February 15, 1852. His particular order of oblates was organized to set sail toward Texas shores in the late months of 1849, but plans changed. All the priests had been pulled out of Texas and returned to France by the first months of 1851. Now the Catholic Church wanted to make another try at this missionary field so far away from home.

Pierre Keralum sailed with a group of young oblates from France in March 1852. After a long trip of pitching up and down on the waves, their ship made it to Galveston in May of that year, and the young priests began their work in this strange new land. The carpenter, Keralum, had instructions to establish the first college-level Catholic seminary in Galveston.

By March 1853, Pierre Keralum received instructions to move to Brownsville. As he rode his donkey along the Rio Grande, he got the first sight of where he would work for the rest of his life as a circuit rider and architect. This flat, open land looked very different from his native France with its Pyrenees and Alps mountains jutting upward. His mission center, situated in Roma, Texas, covered a large area with many families to visit in the following years. In the town of Roma, Pierre did get to design and build the parish church whose cornerstone was laid in September 1854.

A much larger church in Brownsville was incomplete when its oblate superior drowned at sea in August 1856. The church authorities asked Keralum to modify the plans and oversee the completion of this building also. It became the Immaculate Conception Church, dedicated in June 1859.

Although Keralum sometimes drew diagrams of buildings, he was more likely riding his donkey to visit his missionary circuit, which included the countryside upstream from Brownsville. Since Keralum was a true circuit-riding priest, he visited from 70 to 120 ranches in his parish three times a year. Once he came to a home or community, he would preach, catechize, baptize, hear confessions and marry any couples that had been waiting for his appearance. As brilliant a man as Keralum appeared to be, he was unpretentious. He seemed to prefer the simple life of a priest, and the Mexican people found him to be genuine and easy to know.

Keralum had been instructed that his parish was technically on the U. S. side of the border, but he often strayed across to the Mexican side of the Rio Grande administering to the needs of people. He definitely spent some time on Mexican soil in 1865 because it was reported that he held a revival there.

What time Father Keralum was not riding his donkey along the Rio Grande, the officials of the church had him drawing architectural plans for more buildings in Brownsville. He drew the plans, as well as used his carpentry skills in building a nuns' convent, priests' houses and college buildings in that community. By 1872, his age of 55 had taken a toll on his body. Keralum was suffering from failing heath and eyesight, but he continued to visit the little towns in his parish. Keralum's superiors did not want him to ride alone anymore, but he brushed off their concerns and continued to aim his surrey or donkey along the river.

His final trip among his parishioners started November 9, 1872. Some people saw him at a ranch north of the present town of Mercedes, but he never made it to his next destination. Although many people loved the padre, the authorities suspected foul play in his disappearance. Search as they might, his friends never found his body the year he died. It was not until ten years later that some cowboys found his remains with his missionary belongings undisturbed. There were still no definite clues as to how he died. Keralum was interred at the Church of the Immaculate Conception in Brownsville. Some of his remains were placed in a cemetery in Mercedes but were later removed to the Oblate's Provincial Cemetery in San Antonio.

Claude Marie Dubuis, the second bishop of Galveston, wanted more priests to come to Texas. He shared similar feelings with Keralum about the shortage of Catholic fathers, so he traveled to France to recruit more priests for Texas. While he was there, he ordained a twenty-three-year-old priest named Claude Jaillet. Claude then set sail for Texas September 25, 1866, along with several other priests and twelve nuns.

Father Jaillet came first to Galveston and then served at Corpus Christi. He moved to San Diego, Texas, where he helped build a chapel and became the first priest in that community. Church leaders eventually sent him to far West Texas where he served in the Fort Stockton and Fort Davis area in 1871. Jaillet moved about quite frequently as he served next at the churches in San Antonio and Laredo.

Jaillet preferred to ride his horse to the different ranches and serve Catholics that lived far from a town. The church was pleased with his service and wanted to honor Jaillet, but he resisted. He twice refused the office of Bishop. He also intended to refuse other titles the church gave him, but he was too busy to decline. The real title given to Jaillet that suited him best was "saddlebag priest of the Nueces." He spent his later years around Corpus Christi where he died in 1929.

A priest named Pairier also found his way to the Lone Star State. When Catholic circuit rider Father Mathurin Pairier came to Texas in 1869, his life as a priest had been packed with interesting events for twenty years. He had a busy time as a padre before he came to this rugged state of Texas and roamed among the cactus and open plains of Tejas country. His childhood home was in the Diocese of Rennes, France, where he was born in 1822. By 1849 Pairier completed his training and became a member of the Marist Society. He jumped on board a ship from there to sail to New Zealand to do mission work. When he thought the ship would never find land, this distant country finally came into view.

Father Pairier worked in New Zealand, and possibly Australia, for about twenty years in the missions before he got his orders to appear in Texas. Pairier's first position was serving the Catholics in St. Mary's Cathedral at Galveston around 1869. He was sent next to a mission in open ranges and sparsely populated regions.

The padre made his way across the vast expanse of Texas and prayed for the soldiers in Fort Belknap and Fort Griffin, his next location. This able traveler also provided the first Catholic service in Fort Worth in 1870. Two years later, Pairier moved to Dallas and held services in the Odd Fellows' Hall. Eventually, he pushed his parish members to organize a real church building in Dallas. He dedicated the Sacred Heart Church on the first Sunday in August 1873.

At this post, he was among fairly civilized humans living close together, but Pairier's next move placed him in remote West Texas. In 1874 he was stationed at Fort Davis, some four hundred miles south of Fort Worth.

For two years he served the soldiers in the rugged canyons and open spaces between the Davis Mountains. For his next assignment, the Padre was sent to Fort Stockton, but his district stretched as far East as San Angelo. Eventually, the Catholic Church moved him to Mason from 1877 to 1882. This district included Ben Ficklin, Fort Concho, Fort McKavett and Menardville. Father Pairier had a circuit, a big one.

Mathurin Pairier was a striking figure who roamed West Texas as a servant of God in his hack pulled with mules. He was too rotund, weighing about 300 pounds, to ride a grainfed pony, so he rode in his hack. This little buggy, donated by a friend named Phillip Lee, had a top of white canvas to protect him from the scorching Texas sun. The padre did quite well bouncing along the Texas trails with his two small Spanish mules. They delivered him to the various parishes and forts where people were eager to hear the padre preach.

When the jovial Pairier could be seen coming over the hill toward town, people would say, "Father Pairier's hack is coming." His arrival was great news to all people, according to the *San Angelo Standard Times*, May 1924. It told how those who were members of his church as well as those of other faiths and the unbelievers loved him.

The padre preached and listened to confessions by his congregation, but he saw little gold during his ministry. The Mexican families might say to him, *"No tiene dinero,"* meaning they had no money. Instead of receiving gold coins, Father Pairier would have his buggy loaded with corn, beans, pumpkins, melons, chickens or goats by the time he left a village.

Sometimes a priest needed real money to carry on the Lord's work. He would enter Fort Concho or Fort Stockton on payday with his hack full of fresh vegetables. The soldiers spent their pay on his produce, and Pairier had real coins to repair a church's roof or buy medicine for a poor, sick parishioner.

This minister of the Lord was one of the most colorful of all God's circuit riders. His favorite garment was a flaming red flannel undershirt, which could be seen a hundred yards away as he bounced over the prairie toward another village. Although Pairier camped alone many a night, nobody ever seemed to bother him.

Pairier preached wherever he could because many small villages had no church. He preached in a barn near Leedale, a site about eight miles southwest of present-day San Angelo in Tom Green County. The C. D. Metcalfe family owned this "house of God." The congregation that worshipped in the barn represented several denominations.

Knowing the need for a house of worship, Mrs. Elizabeth B. Taylor charged $1 for a lot she donated to the Catholic Church. This land was to be located in Ben Ficklin town near the banks of the Concho River, which was close to Leedale. He already had a small congregation in Leedale. Father Pairier believed that he would finally have a church house in which to read God's word and say the sacraments.

The little community of Ben Ficklin, the county seat of Tom Green, included an impressive courthouse, a stage line started by Ben Ficklin and his partners F. C. Taylor and W. S. Kelly, as well as numerous farms that provided vegetables and hay.

Mother Nature had another idea about building at Ben Ficklin, however. In 1882, the Concho River rose to a frightening level that washed away houses and people in the little town. Even the courthouse disappeared. Logs, boards and some chicken coops floated down the raging river.

Father Pairier felt that a church could still be built in Tom Green County. He was determined to build that church, so he busily pushed for a site in nearby San Angelo, a community that had developed across the Concho River from Fort Concho. Through the help of a group of Catholic parishioners, the Padre found another church site.

He received the deed for a block of lots in nearby San Angelo that included an area bounded on the north by Carolina Street, on the east by Oakes, on the south by Beauregard and the west by Chadbourne Streets. This space became known as "Catholic Block." By 1884 builders started on a church, but the courthouse was being built at the same time, so progress was slow on the Sacred Heart Sanctuary.

Father Pairier watched the county courthouse take shape, but he knew that occasionally the workers were laid off because they had a shortage of stone, sand, lime or lumber. At this time he urged them to help on his church. Since so many of the stonecutters, masons and laborers were German, Irish or Mexican, Pairier knew they would help with the Catholic Church. Sometimes funds for the project were low, so Father Pairier would visit the gambling houses on Concho Street. He could spot the winners and ask them for a donation. Pairier and Rev. Andrew Jackson Potter had a lot in common. They knew how to get some questionable characters to donate money to build churches. After urging laborers to help and begging money, Father Pairier, plus many other Catholics, saw the new church finished in 1885.

An article in the *San Angelo Standard Times*, of October 4, 1885, paid tribute to Father Pairier and the building by saying, "A handsome Roman

The first Catholic Church in San Angelo, built in 1885. Father Pairier raised funds for its construction. Courtesy of the West Texas Collection Library of Angelo State University, San Angelo, Texas.

Catholic Church of red sandstone was the first completed church edifice of the town; a monument to the patience and energy of Father Pairier crowns the finest sight in town. The estimated value is between forty and fifty thousands dollars."

This hard-working padre was not content to have a new church. He wanted a school for the children also. Every year he sent a request to the Sisters of Charity of the Incarnate Word of San Antonio concerning teachers. Every year they told him they wanted to fulfill his request, but they were short of nuns who could teach. As Father Pairier's health declined, Rev. John Sheehan took his place as priest of the San Angelo area.

Maurin Pairier, builder of many churches and congregations, died in 1886 in San Antonio. He did not live to see a Catholic school built in San Angelo, but in August 1887, four sisters left San Antonio traveling westward by train. They arrived in San Angelo and established Immaculate Conception School starting with twenty pupils. Pairier's request had been finally granted. This first house of learning was held in a tiny adobe building with three rooms.

Another Catholic padre found himself transported from civilization to the wide-open stretches of Texas. Father Nicholas Brockdus Eaaken, born in Belguim in 1861, became a circuit-riding priest in the Big Bend area in 1892. If Bloys was the first man to ride the range hunting for sinners in those mountains, Father Brockdus was a close second. His territory ranged from Fort Davis to the Rio Grande, a distance of 133 miles. His first parish church was in Fort Davis, and he ministered to people in nearby Alpine although they had no church building.

That was no problem because Brockdus used Mr. Green Haver's house as a church. In 1900 Alpine finally laid the groundwork and had a church building of their own, Our Lady of Peace Catholic Church. From Alpine, the padre often headed his horse south toward the border.

When he made a journey to the Lajitas area, Brockdus knew he would be traveling a three-day journey one way with his horses and surrey. Some would say it was a long trip, but the Father did not complain. He also made an eighty-five-mile trip to Terlingua, about thirty miles east of Lajitas. Making this journey meant the padre would spend one night or more sleeping out under the stars. He brought with him on the trail a bedroll of two blankets rolled up in canvas, his coffee pot and a little food.

Since Brockdus made the same trip so often, he kept meeting some teamsters pulling their wagons. Some of these men carried supplies to remote ranches, and others were affiliated with the mercury mines of Terlingua. In the mid-1880s, the Marfa and Mariposa mining camp changed its name to Terlingua. By 1902 two or three hundred Mexican laborers recovered the mercury from holes gouged out of the ground. By 1910, the town had a post office, company doctor, erratic telephone service and a good water supply. This town increased to a thousand inhabitants by 1913. The padre saw this change in the economy of this area as he ministered to the swelling number of people.

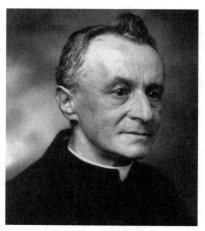

Father Nicholas Brockdus preached to people along the Rio Grande. Courtesy of the Harry Ransom Humanities Research Center, University of Texas at Austin

Whenever they could, the freighters, hauling supplies in their wagons, tried to camp with the padre. They could share the fire as well as the visiting. He made these long trips every three or four months. Brockdus started traveling to the border in 1900, and he kept up this schedule for thirty years. After many months of making this journey in a surrey, Brockdus finally bought a Model T Ford. He continued to meet his congregations as he bounced over the rough roads and neared the age of seventy.

His parishioners knew he was coming to Terlingua or Lajitas because Brockdus sent his messages ahead of him by the local *avisadores*. They were men who could send long-distance messages by bouncing sunlight off a shiny surface similar to a mirror. The signalers who sent these messages stood on elevated hills to flash the message from one hill to another.

By the time the padre reached the villages, the people had assembled and were ready to worship with the circuit rider. His parishioners came down from the mountains on both sides of the Rio Grande and worshiped with Brockdus.

Avisadores, as a way of sending messages, had been used over much of the Tejas country even before the Texas War for Independence. W. D. Smithers, a Texas photographer and writer, interviewed an elderly man named Vargas in 1907. This Zapotec Indian served with the Mexican troops at San Antonio in 1836. He said that when the Mexican Army was defeated at San Jacinto, he knew of the battle soon after it happened. *Avisadores* sent the message from San Jacinto to San Antonio in a few minutes by bouncing light off a mirror, from mountain to mountain.

Now years later, the messengers were still at work. When Brockdus started his trips to Lajitas, he was probably surprised to see about five hundred people ready to worship with him when he arrived. They were coming to worship God in a community with no church. The Padre discussed the problem of needing a house of worship to his parishioners during the next months. Eventually Mexican men built small churches in Terlingua and Lajitas by using adobe bricks that they were able to construct very efficiently. A few dollars of real money were spent only for lumber to make the doors and two windows in each church. The merchants in Alpine and Fort Davis donated most of the money for these items.

Brockdus was very aware of the turbulent times his people experienced while living along the border. Pancho Villa and his bandits raided any community that had goods he needed to carry on his war. He even killed American mining engineers while they were aboard trains stopped in Chihuahua. President Wilson finally consented to send American troops to be stationed along the border to protect U. S. citizens.

After increased raids by Villa in 1916, the U. S. government increased its number of troops along the border. This was an attempt to stop the aggression and stop the smuggling of arms across the border. The Rio Grande had eventually eleven cavalry posts along its waters: Boquillas, Glenn Springs, Terlingua, Lajitas, Redford, Presidio, India, Ruidosa, Candelaria, Holland's Camp and Evett's Ranch. These places were scattered along the Rio Grande both upstream and downstream from Lajitas.

Most of these camps were home to at least 75 to 100 soldiers. Holland Camp was much larger for it included enough cavalry troopers, infantrymen, scouts, guides, and pack train personnel to total 400 men.

People living at Glenn Springs, on the Father's circuit, woke up May 5, 1916, to the thunder of horses' hooves pounding down the road.

Mexican raiders under Rodriguez Ramirez's and Natividad Alvarez's leadership attacked their town. The village's defense, the nine soldiers of Troop A of the Fourteenth Cavalry, were heavily outnumbered by the Mexican raiders. The soldiers left their tents under fire and hid in an adobe building. When the raiders set the building on fire, three of the troopers died and four others were wounded.

Still Father Brockdus ministered to the people and hoped for calmer times. Lack of schools in this isolated area was another problem that bothered Brockdus. He worked hard to bring education to these isolated places and finally saw a school built in Glenn Springs in 1929. He also helped to build a school at the Johnson Ranch in 1932. There were five students attending this second house of learning, but the school closed after two years because no other teacher wanted to live in an area so isolated as this one some 120 miles from Alpine. To make matters worse, the students ranged in age from seven to sixteen, and they spoke no English. Language was not the worst barrier. The new teacher discovered quickly that these boys and girls had never darkened the door of a schoolhouse before. They did not understand what the teacher was trying to accomplish.

As the padre ministered to the people along the border, he noticed how the Spanish people made their livelihood. The art of wax-making was very common and productive in this area. In fact, the Glenn Springs area had the biggest factory in the United States that made their wax from the Candelilla plant.

When the Mexicans gathered the long-stemmed plants, they separated the wax from the stems by heating the plants in a mixture of sulfuric acid. Wax separated and floated to the top of the liquid.

Brockdus finally stopped his long journeys to the border in 1930, but he did not stop preaching. The padre devoted his next thirteen years to his church at Fort Davis. This congregation represented the parish where he started his ministry in 1892. He worked tirelessly to reach isolated families in this sparsely populated area and worked miracles in the process.

Priests traveled the Rio Grande and the fort trails of Texas many years before the Panhandle of Texas was settled. This northwestern section of the Lone Star State was the last hold-out for raiding bands of Indians. At this time, some daring priests from Kansas and New Mexico would venture into that part of Texas. Otherwise, it was no-man's-land until railroads and settlers moved that direction around 1875. The Fort Worth and Denver Railway's tracks crossed the wide, open spaces of this region in 1887.

Priests from the Gainsville area made their way to this new frontier. They soon discovered that this region had a lot of Irish and German railroad employees who were Catholic. With a ready-made congregation, Catholics built St. Mary's at Clarendon in 1892, the first Catholic Church in the Panhandle.

As the years passed, the Oblate priests used new ways to visit their parishioners in the early 1900s. The advent of trains made travel much nicer for God's messengers. They could leave their headquarters in San Antonio and travel to Central Texas and eventually to the Panhandle.

Father Yves Tymen traveled in the opposite direction from the Panhandle as he moved toward Texas's southeastern counties. He used a strange-looking vehicle for his trips into the Texas Valley region in 1913. He called his wheels the "St. Peter Chapel Car." It was rigged so it had sleeping facilities for two people, or if he enlarged it with his tent, the car became a little chapel. Tymen was far ahead in planning a car that looked much like recreational vehicles of today.

This same order of priests helped Mexican-American workers with minimum wage problems and schools for their children. This group, called the "Cavalry of Christ on the Rio Grande," left their mark of kindness and help.

While padres tried to bring Christianity to the banks of the Rio Grande, other men tried to bring the law to a lawless country. Men on both sides of this river were known to slip cattle across the river in the "dark of the moon." John Riley Bannister was a lawman who spent many hours in the saddle along the Rio Grande. Officially he was called a treasury agent assigned to help police the Mexican border against cattle smuggling in 1892. Later he carried the title of inspector for the Texas Cattle Raisers Association. He originated the field-inspection service for the association and was its first chief. As his fame was recognized, Bannister's services were needed to investigate cattle rustling in New Mexico, Kansas, and Oklahoma, as well as Texas. In 1914, he hung up his spurs, so to speak, and took "an easy job" as sheriff in Coleman County.

By this time, there were fewer lawless people along the Rio Grande, so more people attended churches than before the padres came. People like Bannister tried to help people live by the Ten Commandments that the padres preached.

As the nineteenth century closed, people in Texas no longer needed circuit-riding preachers. Churches sprang up in all the communities and towns, so that families could now enjoy worshipping with their neighbors. Better transportation made it easier for parents to bring their children into town to hear the preacher rather than depend on the parson coming to their house. The fear of Indians and outlaws on the loose diminished, so travelers no longer worried about the trails that circuit riders traversed across Texas.

Although these days of pistol packin' preachers are gone, their legacy lives on. These parsons fought for Texas's independence, trailed cattle to points northward and plowed the soil while finding time to break the bread of life for their fellow Texans. Other men of God taught school, served as doctors and entered politics so they could help citizens of this great state. Early-day preachers and padres left their mark on Texas.

READING ABOUT
PISTOL PACKIN' PREACHERS

Anderson, J. W. *From the Plains to the Pulpit*. Goose Creek, Texas: Anderson & Sons. 1907.

Austin, Stephen F. "Description of Texas." *Southwestern Historical Quarterly*, Vol. 2, 215.

Baker, Inez. *Yesterday in Hall County*. Memphis, Texas: 1940.

Baker, Robert A. *The Blossoming Desert—A Concise History of Texas Baptists*. Waco: Word Books, 1970.

Barr, Alwyn and Calvert, Robert A., eds. *Black Leaders: Texans for Their Times*. Austin: Texas State Historical Association, 1981.

Barr, Alwyn. *Black Texans: A History of Negroes in Texas, 1528–1971*. Austin: Jenkins, 1973.

Baugh, C. *Border Skylines: Fifty Years of "Tallying Out" on the Bloys Round-up Grounds*. Dallas, [c1940].

Beard, Richard. *Brief Biographical Sketches of Some of the Early Ministers of the Cumberland Presbyterian Church,* 2nd Series. Nashville: Cumberland Board of Publication, 1874.

Blakely, Mike. *Wild Camp Tales*. Plano: Republic of Texas Press, 1995.

Blasig, Anne. *The Wends of Texas*. San Antonio: Naylor, 1954; rpt., Brownsville: Springman-King Printing, 1981.

Bogener, Steve. "The World Heavyweight Boxing Championship Bout, 1896, at Langtry, Texas." *West Texas Historical Association Year Book, Vol. LXXIV*. Lubbock: Texas Tech University Press, 1998.

Boren, Carter E. *Religion on the Texas Frontier*. San Antonio: Naylor Co., 1968.

Brackenridge, R. Douglas. *Voice in the Wilderness*. San Antonio: Trinity University Press, 1968.

Bradley, Willo M. Robinson and Robinson, Edith Lucille. *Family Trails: Ancestral & Contemporary*. Stephenville, Texas: Stephenville Printing Co., 1978.

Brezosky, Lynn. "Rather Sleep in Texas." *San Angelo Standard Times,* June 1, 2003, 1A.

Browder, Virginia. *Donley County: Land O' Promise.* Wichita Falls, Texas: Nortex, 1975.

Burroughs, Jean M. *On the Trail: The Life and Tales of "Lead Steer" Potter.* Santa Fe: Museum of New Mexico Press, 1980.

Caldwell, Lillie Moerbe. *Texas Wends: Their First Half-Century.* Salado, Texas: Anson Jones Press, 1961.

Carroll, James Milton. *A History of Texas Baptists.* Dallas: Baptist Standard Printing, 1923.

Chronicles of Our Heritage, Vol 1. Abilene: Chapman & Sons, 2003.

"Comanche and the Hardin Gang." *Southwestern Historical Quarterly,* Vol. 67, 55.

Cooley, Nancy V. "Special Deputy to the Almighty." *Texas Parade,* November 1972.

County Historical Commission. *San Saba County History.* San Saba, Texas: 1983.

Cubstead, Lane. "The Firm Foundation, 1884–1957: The History of a Pioneer Religious Journal and Its Editors." M.A. thesis, University of Texas, 1957.

Dawson, J. M. D.D. *The Spiritual Conquest of the Southwest.* Nashville: Baptist Sunday School Board, 1927

Dixie Babbs. Unpublished "Autobiography of Dixie Babbs."

Dobie, J. Frank. *Cow People.* Boston: Little Brown & Company, 1964.

Doyon, Bernard. *The Cavalry of Christ on the Rio Grande, 1849–1883.* Milwaukee: Bruce, 1956.

Drago, Gail & Ruff, Ann. *Outlaws in Petticoats.* Plano: Republic of Texas Press, 1995.

"Father Pairier." Vertical File. West Texas Collection, Angelo State University Library, San Angelo, Texas.

Ferguson, Bennie and Hatfield, Dot Ferguson. "Not Ready to Die." *Texas Highways,* March 2003.

Flippin, Perry. "Spooky visage greets fort visitor." *San Angelo Standard Times,* August 26, 2003, 5A.

Fontaine, Jacob III, and Burd, Gene. *Jacob Fontaine.* Austin: Eakin Press, 1983.

"Fort Bend County." Vertical Files. Texas History Center, University of Texas at Austin.

"Frank J. Kiefer." *Texas Baptist Herald,* October 12, 19, 1876; February 26, 1880; January 26, 1882; August 14, 1889; June 18, 1890.

Gravis, Rev. Peter W. *Twenty-five Years on the Outside Row.* Brownwood: Cross Timber Press. 1966.

Grose, Charles Williams. "Black Newspapers in Texas, 1868–1970." Ph.D. dissertation. University of Texas at Austin, 1972.

Grossman, Lori. "Travis' Son." *Texas Highways,* March 2003.

Haislet, John A., ed. *Famous Trees of Texas.* College Station: Texas Forest Service, 1970; 3d ed., 1984.

Hambrick, Alma Ward. *The Call of San Saba: A History of San Saba County.* San Antonio: Naylor, 1941; 2d ed., Austin Jenkins, 1969.

Holworthy, Sister Mary Xavier. *Father Jaillet: Saddlebag Priest of the Nueces.* Corpus Christi: Incarnate Word Academy, 1948.

Hunter, J. Marvin. *The Story of Lottie Deno, Her Life and Times.* Bandera, Texas, 1959.

———. *The Trail Drivers of Texas.* New York: Argosy-Antiquarian LTD, 1963.

Irion County Historical Society. *Irion County History.* San Angelo: Anchor Publishing Co., 1978.

Jones, Gene. Conversation with author, Christoval, Texas, April 14, 2004.

Justice, Glenn. *Little Known History of the Texas Big Bend.* Odessa: Rimrock Press, 2001.

Laine, Tanner. *Cow Country.* Hereford: Pioneer Book Publishers, Inc., 1969.

Langford, Bertie. Telephone conversation with the author, 22 October 2003.

Lewis, Willie Newbury. *Between Sun and Sod.* Clarendon, Texas: Clarendon Press, 1938.

Marohn, Richard C. *The Last Gunfighter, John Wesley Hardin.* College Station, Texas: Creative Publishing Company, 1995.

McSwain, Ross. *Tales From Out Yonder.* Plano: Republic of Texas Press, 2001.

Morrell, Z. N. *Flowers and Fruits in the Wilderness.* St. Louis: Commercial Printing Company, 1972.

Neville, A. W. *The Red River Then and Now.* Paris, Texas: North Texas Publishing Company.

Noble, Harry P., Jr. "Rev. Sumner Bacon." *San Augustine Tribune.* 3 articles in June 1993.

Pettijohn, Mary Jane, granddaughter of Choctaw Bill Robinson and her daughter, Patsy Means, conversation with author, Comanche, Texas, 25 October 2003.

Phares, Ross. *Bible in Pocket, Gun in Hand.* New York: Doubleday and Co., 1964.

Quartermaster Reports from Fort Chadbourne, 1856 to 1860.

"Religious Journal and Its Editors." M.A. thesis, University of Texas, 1957.

Rooney, Sister M. Nellie. "A History of the Catholic Church in the Panhandle-Plains Area of Texas from 1875 to 1916." M. A. thesis, Catholic University of America, 1954.

Smithers, W. D. *Circuit Riders of the Big Bend.* El Paso: Texas Western Press, 1981.

Spencer, Tim, Elisha Hoffman, Anthony Showalter. "Circuit-Ridin' Preacher." Copyrighted 1954 by Manna Music, Inc.

Stokes, Katy. *Paisano, Story of a Cowboy and a Camp Meeting.* Waco: Texian Press, 1980.

Sullivan, W. J. L. *Twelve Years in the Saddle for Law & Order on the Frontiers of Texas.* New York: Buffalo–Head Press, 1966.

"The Real Story of the Alamo." TV History Channel, December 21, 2003.

Tijerina, Andres. *Tejanos and Texas Under the Mexican Flag, 1821–1836*. College Station: Texas A&M Press, 1994.

Tolbert, Frank X. *An Informal History of Texas*. New York: Harper & Brothers, 1951.

Tom Green County Historical Preservation League, Inc. *Tom Green County Chronicles of our Heritage,* Vol 1. Abilene: Chapman & Sons, 2003.

United Methodist Church Collection, West Texas Collection, Angelo State University, San Angelo, Texas.

Urbantke, Carl. *Texas Is the Place for Me*. Austin: The Pemberton Press, 1970.

Vinson, Doris. Telephone conversation with author, Mertzon, Texas, 22 October 2003.

Wallis, George A. *Cattle Kings of the Staked Plains*. Dallas: American Guild Press, 1957.

Walter, N. Vernon, Sledge, Robert W., Monk, Robert C., and Spellman, Norman W. *The Methodist Excitement in Texas*. Dallas: The Texas United Methodist Historical Society, 1984.

Ward, Geoffrey C. *The West, An Illustrated History*. Boston: Little, Brown, and Company, 1996.

Webb, Walter Prescott. *The Texas Rangers*. Austin: University of Texas Press, 1935.

Wiley, Rosa Lee. *History of Van Horn and Culberson County, Texas*. Hereford: Pioneer Book Publishers, Inc., 1973.

William Stewart. *The Texas Colonists and Religion, 1821–1836*. Austin: Baldwin & Sons, 1924.

Wood, W. D. "History of Leon County." *Southwestern Historical Quarterly,* Vol. 14, 215, 216.

INDEX